FREEDOM IN CREDIT CARDS

HOW TO TAKE CHARGE OF YOUR LIFE, YOUR CREDIT, AND YOUR FUTURE

FREEDOM IN CREDIT CARDS

HOW TO TAKE CHARGE OF YOUR LIFE, YOUR CREDIT, AND YOUR FUTURE

BY

LUCCIANO A. DÍAZ-SKOFF

NEW DEGREE PRESS

FREEDOM IN CREDIT CARDS
How to Take Charge of Your Life, Your Credit, and Your Future

ISBN   978-1-63676-326-2   *Paperback*
          978-1-63676-327-9   *Kindle Ebook*
          978-1-63676-328-6   *Ebook*

Table of Contents

To my mom and dad,
for everything.

Open Letter to Readers

We all have heard something about credit cards, from your friends, your parents, or a video that popped up on the internet. The videos and the gurus talked about maximizing points, sign up bonuses, credit card churning, and much more. It turns out that building information, maintaining, and growing your credit is not that precise. You will find cards for beginners or cards for traveling, but you will hardly find data on when to apply for your next card and when to not.

I am writing this book because I went through that same struggle. I was trying to find a game plan on how to build credit. No plan could start me out with credit until I sat down and understood what credit is. This book is my journey from a nonexistent credit score to seven hundred fifty-plus across all three credit bureaus in a year. Now my credit portfolio has four credit cards and more than $10,000 in available credit. By the end of writing this book, I'll be in the process (again) of buying my first home.

I'm a real guy playing the credit game. I post regularly on Instagram (@LuccianoDiazSkoff), and I write for everyone learning about credit on my page at Luccian-oDiazSkoff.com. I also want to hear from you and get a glimpse of your credit story. Let's try this: Send me an email at Lucciano@FreedomInCreditCards.com with the subject line, "Started playing the game" and share with me two things:

- What made you decide to start building credit today?
- What do you want to achieve with your credit?

It would bring me great joy to hear from you about your credit experience and how you applied the material in this book to change your life. I know talking about money can be an emotional matter to most. That is translated to credit cards also. We have all heard misconceptions about credit cards that have shaped how we think about them. Those misconceptions then turn into scripts repeated by family and friends and change your behavior toward credit. Those scripts can influence your decisions for life. I'm sure these scripts sound familiar:

- "Having a lot of cards is bad for your credit."
- "Too many cards mean you have a lot of debt."
- "Credit cards are the worst."
- "Never take out a credit card. They will ruin you."
- "You should have one or two credit cards, but no more than that."
- "Why do you need so many credit cards?"
- "Credit cards have no benefit."
- "You should cut all your credit cards up and forget about them."

I know all the emotions you feel when applying for your first card and being denied over and over again. (I still get excited when applying for a new card.) Enjoy the feeling of getting your first credit card approval and again with your second, third, and fourth card. I celebrate every time I get a new credit card approval. I know the feeling of checking my FICO score almost daily to see how I'm growing. I checked my bank account every weekend to pay the statement—being scared of the late fees or of missing a payment. Trust me, those emotions will subside. Once you get the game flowing, you will be in charge of your credit score and credit cards.

"Don't cut up your credit cards, the problem is not the cards, it's the lack of financial literacy of the person holding the cards."
—ROBERT KIYOSAKI

I hope this book gets you as excited about credit as I am writing it. I hope you feel that every card application is a new opportunity to grow your credit. Let this book be a tool to build and grow your credit, your way. Use this book to start your journey toward financial freedom.

CHAPTER 1.

Invisible Elephants

———

"Financial Freedom is freedom from fear."

—*ROBERT KIYOSAKI*

Every Friday after work, I join a couple of friends for beers over at Bar La Penúltima in Santurce, Puerto Rico, a very nice, low-key spot to decompress over one of their famous cocktails and tasty burgers. This is a place where we can relax, share ideas and thoughts, and disconnect from work. We often find ourselves talking about everything except one topic: money. The reason is because they are scared about what they will find or because they do not know what to do with their money.

I think money should be a crucial topic of conversation between friends—how you're handling your income, what you're investing in, how your savings look, and the like. I noticed people hate to talk about and have negative experiences with credit cards. Yeah, that plastic thing that you see being thrown around whenever the bill comes? They fear what they think credit cards mean, but everyone wants the points.

Once I noticed this behavior with my friends, I tried it out with my colleagues. We went out for a dinner celebration after the closing presentation of a project phase. I proposed the question of what a good credit card is to start my credit history. Very quickly, one responded: "Forget about that, credit cards will lead you to your ruin. Don't have more than two. That has worked for my parents."

A second friend concurred and said he only had one from college. Surprised by their reaction, I looked up how to start credit and how the credit game is played.

A couple of months after being denied for a loan by the bank, my first credit card was approved. Getting approved wasn't that hard. My local bank, Banco Popular de Puerto Rico, took around fifteen days to decide since I had no credit history. With an excellent credit score, banks can approve you in sixty seconds.[1] You see the difference in having and not having a credit score, right? They just needed proof of work, a.k.a. employee contract or letter, and the last two deposits in my bank account. At last, my first credit card! It was a Premia card with a sign-up bonus and a points program. Not bad to start my journey.

Some days later, I joined two close friends, Angel Cintrón and Iván Cirino, at the bar to show them my achievement. They were cheerful and asked how I did it. I was happy to share the process. "First, see what local banks or credit unions you could easily approve with. Then, ask them what requirements and documents are needed. Lastly, give them what they need, and *voilà,* my first credit card."

---

1   LaToya Irby, "Find out How Long It Takes to Get Approved for a Credit Card," The Balance, June 14, 2020.

I also told them how I was able to start with two credit cards instead of one. Yes, you read that right. Angel was as surprised as you. "Wait, you said two cards? How did you manage to do that? They only approve you for one."

Well, I did not know if it was an error of the bank representative, or if this is a policy they do not practice often. When the credit limit was approved, the representative showed me three cards to choose from. A simple cashback card, where they would give me 1.5 percent cash per every $1 spent. Not bad, actually—Chase has a similar product. The second card was a Premia rewards where I would accumulate points instead of cash back, much like Chase's Ultimate Reward points or Amex's Membership Reward points. And the third card accumulated miles the same way the other two cards accumulated cash back or points.

When sitting down with the representative looking at cards, you might feel a rush or pressure to pick a card quickly and be done. In reality, you are in the middle of a negotiation. You see, the bank has already approved your credit limit and they already have you in their database. You are almost theirs. At the same time, they need new customers so they can keep their business going. On your part, your credit has already been pulled. That inquiry, whether you get a card or not, will stay in your report for two years. Better make the best of it.

Before deciding, and in true Lucciano fashion, I asked José, the bank representative, what was the best card they had (not the one they could offer me). I wanted to take my chances with their best product. José then showed me a Black Dual card where I would get two credit cards with the same account. One was a Visa card and the other an American Express card, in case a place did not take one or the other. The best part: they were black, and I would have two of them. Sadly, José told me that I couldn't get that card because it was reserved for people with credit lines of $10,000 or more. I had been approved for a third of that. A bit discouraged, a random thought crossed my mind: I want two credit cards. I do not know why or how, but If I couldn't get the black card, I wanted two cards. I also knew that starting with two credit cards would help boost my credit score. So I told José, "Well, what is the best you can do for me? Can I get two cards then?" "Sure," he said. Amazed with his answer, I laughed and asked with skepticism, "Really?" José responded, "Sure, you can choose any two and let me know what their limits would be."

At this point, I was having a party in my head. I was approved for a $3,000 credit limit and I could start my credit journey with two credit cards. How amazing is that! I was so distracted from my excitement that I did not hesitate and chose the cards I would be using more: the Premia card with points to redeem, and the miles card. (Yes, yes, I know, this was pre-pandemic where we could fly around the world without wearing masks and quarantining for fourteen days. At least I'm racking up enough miles to fly anywhere in the world for free.)

I was happy to finally start playing the game, and my friends were too. Angel and Iván congratulated me on the achievement and ordered a round of drinks. As the conversation kept going, I mentioned that in about six months I would get another card. That is when Iván stops me and says, "You're fine with two cards. You do not need another card."

I debated his point, telling him many different cards on the market help in different ways. One card gives you points you can redeem for special offers in restaurants. Another card matches your spending in the year as cashback. Another card gives you miles you can use to fly for free. Credit cards are a tool most people are missing out on.

However, more than 189 million Americans have credit cards. The average credit card holder has at least four cards. On average, each household with a credit card carries $8,398 in credit card debt. The total US consumer debt is at $13.86 trillion.[2]

My friends mentioned the 2008 market crash, when people got scared and concerned about credit, and how another recession might come. They argued that having numerous cards is bad for your credit. But this is a huge misconception! The more cards you have, the higher your credit score. But be careful, because if you do not know how to use them, you could be part of these statistics.

For example, if you have $4,398.00 of debt (roughly half of the average household debt) and only pay the minimum each month (3 percent, assuming you are paying 0 percent interest), you'd be in debt for almost three years. But if you pay 5 percent off each month, roughly $219.90, you'd have the credit card paid off in less than two years. By aggressively paying 10 percent of that debt, $439.80,

2   Ilyce Glink and Samuel J Tamkin, "Perspective | The Key to Escaping from Debt Is to Pay off the Highest Interest Accounts First," The Washington Post, March 13, 2020.

INVISIBLE ELEPHANTS · 17

it will only take you ten months to pay the whole debt. Now, assuming your bank does not give 0 percent on that debt, you'd be paying your debt for three times as long or more in any of the three scenarios. You have to be smart with your credit and your debt.

The national credit score average as of October 2020 is seven hundred eleven, eight more points than last year. [3] Americans age seventy-five and older have an average credit score of seven hundred fifty-eight, forty-seven points higher than the national average. Americans between the ages of fifty-six and seventy-four hold the second-highest FICO Score average of seven hundred thirty-six. People between the ages of forty and fifty-five have an average FICO Score of six hundred ninety-nine, while Americans between the ages of twenty-four and thirty-nine score six hundred eighty on average. The average FICO Score for Americans between the ages of eighteen and twenty-three is six hundred sixty-seven.

This spike in credit score average is due to a couple of reasons. During the 2020 COVID-19 pandemic, consumer debt management has seen a positive reaction. Shrinking debt, drop in delinquencies (late payments), and decreased utilization rates have attributed to the growth in credit scores. Average credit card utilization dropped by 12 percent while delinquencies dropped by another 10 percent.

What does this mean? Older generations tend to have better credit than younger ones because of their time in the game. Why is this important? Because almost a

---

3   Stefan Lembo-Stolba, "What Is the Average Credit Score in the U.S.?" Experian, September 6, 2019.

fourth of millennials do not know their credit score and two-thirds do not own a credit card. This state causes more harm than you think. If you are between the ages of twenty and thirty-nine, or even forty-nine, you are truncating your chances for lower interest rates with that higher credit score. Even having that amount of debt can seriously hurt your chances of getting another loan or line of credit.

I'm telling you this because most people are scared of credit cards. In other words, they do not know how to play the game. The credit card game is one in which everybody wins if played right, not like your typical board games where you have the winner, the runner up, third place, and so on. Even though everyone plays their own game, everyone has the same set of rules. This game is not affected by other players. The only player in control of what happens to you is you. Ultimately, the goal of the game is to have a solid credit score, a handful of credit cards that work for you, and the access to offers normally not accessible with cash. But the game doesn't end there.

Credit cards are the biggest stepping-stone of building credit. Yes, you can start with other credit building products like a personal loan or a student loan. Ultimately, they all work toward the same goal. The cusp of the game is financial freedom; to have enough savings, investments, and money to afford the life we desire. Your credit will help you start building that life early on when you do not have money to buy a home or a car. At the same time, you can travel the world using the best perk of a credit card: its points. You do not need to play the game if you do not want to. That is completely up to you. In any case, do not be scared to work for the life you want.

Around May of 2019, I stepped into a local bank in Puerto Rico looking for a loan to buy a house. For me, at twenty-seven, it was time to buy a place to live instead of renting frequently. After two years of working, hustling, investing, and saving, I had enough down payment for my first home. While going over everything with the bank representative, the best mortgage interest rate he could offer was something close to 7 percent. I screamed internally. I was planning on getting something between 3 percent and 4 percent. But I couldn't. I did not have a credit score. The bank had nothing they could rely on to decide what percentage to give me because they did not know how good a borrower I was. After learning about my nonexistent credit score, I did the only thing I thought I could do: sit down and learn to become a credit expert so I never had to go through that experience again. I focused so hard on knowing everything regarding credit and credit cards for the next six months that I ended up helping three different friends with their own credit score.

I learned four very important things about credit. First, what credit is. For you, it is using the bank's money to make a purchase that you will repay later. For the bank, it is a way of knowing how good you are at borrowing money and paying it back on time. Secondly, and very importantly, how to use it, how to use credit to cover purchases that you do not have the money for at the moment, and how to use that credit in form of credit cards to earn cash-back or miles. Third, how to maintain and grow your credit. You do not want to have a low credit score, because that will leave you out of the best interest deals in the market. Maintaining your credit is important too.

Paying on time, in full, and never carrying a balance are key aspects to keep in mind with your credit.

Lastly, I learned how having credit and a credit score will help you in the future. When you buy a home, they will ask if you want to buy it cashed or financed. For most of us, we will choose the latter. Having a high credit score at this point could hugely benefit you. At the current state, if you were to buy a home and your credit score is above seven hundred sixty, you could be offered an interest rate of 2.377 percent. This is the lowest interest rate for a thirty-year fixed mortgage. But let's say you have a credit score of six hundred thirty-five instead. Not much of a deal, right? Nor the 3.966 percent interest rate you would be offered. You would pay $260 more per month, or $3,120 per year or roughly $93,600 in the lifetime of the loan.[4] Treat your credit as if your money depended on it, because it does.

With this knowledge, I've helped friends consolidate debt, receive a higher credit limit, get inquiries removed from their history, and taught them how to take full advantage of their cards. I've also helped them through their journey of applying and getting approved for their first, second, and third card. In this learning process of reading, watching videos, joining Facebook groups, and sharing information with friends and colleagues, the same debate kept showing up. Credit is good for you; credit is bad for you. You don't need credit because you have cash. If you have too many credit cards, it hurts your score. And so on.

---

4   Megan DeMatteo, "This Is the Credit Score Lenders Use When You Apply for a Mortgage," CNBC, December 2, 2020.

This back and forth of credit being good or bad is not the problem. We often give credit, and money, a moral significance. I'm sure you've heard the quote, "Money is the root of all evil," meaning that money equals evil. It doesn't. Money equals value. Thus, credit isn't good nor bad. Credit is a tool that broadens your horizon. And like any tool, you must know how to use it properly. It will open a world of opportunities that cash simply can't. And with the right mindset, credit cards will become your secret to financial freedom. How do you do that? By knowing how to play the game.

If you are a college student who just got a credit card, a young professional looking for your second card, or just someone who wants to enter the credit game, this book is for you. You will learn how the game is set up, the three rules that will set you up for financial freedom, and how to get the most out of every card.

To get started with credit and credit cards, visit me at LuccianoDiazSkoff.com and reach out on Instagram @ LuccianoDiazSkoff.

CHAPTER 2.

Well, This Is Embarrassing

———

"No river can return to its source, yet all rivers must have a beginning."

—AMERICAN INDIAN PROVERB

I wanted to buy a home. To do that, I needed proof of employment, steady income, and having enough savings. I also needed to know the costs related to buying a house like the down payment, closing costs, mortgage payments and insurance, and property taxes, among other things. The real estate agent was optional for me, but it depends on the deal. You might find property whose seller is the owner, or they might have a real estate agent handling the negotiation, or the other way around. You do not want to go through the hassle of endlessly scrolling by listings or webpages when you can have a realtor do all the work. But they usually charge a 5 percent to 6 percent commission when the house is sold.[5] I had found my dream home without any help. Plus, I wanted the full experience of buying a home.

Now, suppose you find the house you want to buy, and you know you can buy it. In that case, you head down to the bank and talk with a representative about the mortgage, the down payment, the terms you want to buy it under, bonds, insurance, and all other fees you're unaware of. And once you have all that down, they check your credit history, and *voilà,* you have none. You're there, frozen, not even a pulse, and not knowing what to say. You don't understand what has happened. You had it all figured out, but "you do not have a credit history"?

CNBC interviewed Graham Stephan, Youtube star and real estate investor, on the importance of credit. This is what he had to say: "If I could go back and do anything over again, I would get a credit card the day I turned eighteen," because it would have allowed him to start building credit sooner. When he wanted to buy his first property in his early twenties, "even though I had the savings and I had the income, no bank wanted to give me a loan because I had zero credit history."

The first thing most mortgage lenders look at is your credit score, since it's a good indicator of your ability to pay off debt.

What does not having a credit history mean? It means the interest, down payment, insurance, and more are higher because the bank doesn't know if you are good at

---

5   Taylor Gordon, "How Much Is the Average Real Estate Commission?" Ownerly, June 18, 2020.

paying back the money you borrowed. I have been doing business for five years, never had debt, have a college degree in engineering, and have some cash in my savings, but that doesn't show the bank I am good with money. In other words, the bank, even though you have financial experience, does not know how good of a borrower you are. They also don't know how much risk you represent if they were to lend you money. This is what the credit score means. Look at it this way: your credit report is your financial resume.

I asked the representative what I could do. How do I start this so-called credit history, and how much do I need? "You need more than seven hundred twenty to get a good deal, and that would take you around two years." I couldn't believe it. I would lose my dream home in the center of San Juan, Puerto Rico, because I did not have this magic number. I didn't even know where it came from or how it worked.

I appreciated the information from the bank representative, but after feeling heartbroken and defeated, I went home and called my friends to see what they knew about credit. I couldn't understand why I didn't know about this.

Throughout my twenty-seven years of life and over five years owning a business, I never knew or understood the importance of having a credit history. I had always done business with cash. I didn't know about the advantages of credit. Again, I never had any debt; I always paid on time, but I paid in cash. And that's not all: My parents, friends, or school never taught or introduced me to credit. Why was that? I couldn't understand why I never had a compulsory class in school to manage my finances. After all, I was studying to make money and give back to my island.

The school would spit me out into the world at eighteen years old, so I better be prepared for it. In college, there was even a class on the new experiences you would have called "The College Experience." Not a single professor told me I should start thinking about my future financially other than graduate and make sure you get a job (which, of course, looks good on the university's resume).

So, I started thinking that if I was never taught about credit in my education process, then how did any of my friends, if they had credit, know about it? I picked up the phone, and the first friend I asked about it, you wouldn't believe his response, said, "Yes, I have some, but I have seven grand in debt." I responded, "How could that be?" He answered, "Well, I was reckless and did not understand what a credit card was. I regret it now."

"One can either control the use of a credit card or allow the credit card to control you."

—LAMONT PROSPECT

I was astonished. What is this? Why do you have debt? Should I have debt? Having credit cards means having debt? I couldn't believe it. I said, okay, let's try another friend. I called Iván and asked, "Do you have credit?" He answered, "Yes." I said, "Cool. Now, what do you use it for?" He told me, "Nothing. It's the company's credit card."

Again, I was surprised, so I asked him if he had a personal credit card. Iván answered yes, the first and only credit card he got when he started college with a $500 limit. He doesn't even use it.

I was overwhelmed by all this new information, so I took a break and gave my brain time to process what I had just learned. A week later, I was having dinner with another group of friends in Aurorita, the best Mexican restaurant in Puerto Rico since 1973, at least for me. We usually order the *Nachos Chihuahua Special* and the *Burrito de Carnitas Suizo Elefante.* It's just amazing food.

While enjoying our margaritas, it was time to pay. At that moment, Gautam asked, "Who wants the points?" I responded, "Points? What are you talking about?" Gautam said, "Yes, points. This card gives me 3 percent points on all restaurants, even when delivered." I had forgotten everything I had read! So I asked him, "What do you use the points for?" He then told me he was planning a trip with his girlfriend and wanted to pay it completely with credit card points. These are the same points the credit cards give you for using them. You can use the points toward miles, points for cash-back, or free access to something, somewhere, even to buy stuff through the bank's portal. Amazing!

I noticed two other friends were quiet. I asked Andrea and Alma what was up, and then a barrage of opinions started. They went something like this: "Credit cards are bad. You'll end up in debt. I have $2,800 in debt on a single card, and it's killing me. I can't pay it down." Andrea says, "Never have more than two. I don't have that problem because I only have two, and I don't use one." Then, Alma states, "You'll want to spend every penny. I only have two with no more than $500 limit, because then I'll want to spend it." Baffled by their reactions, I wanted to learn more from their situation but couldn't. They were already annoyed talking about their pain. Instead of inquiring, I asked for a recommendation on what should be my first card, to which they both concluded, saying, "Credit cards are bad. You really don't need a credit card. Use cash instead."

Amused at this reaction, I felt the need to do something about it. I needed to know if this was all true. I went back home, opened my computer, and started researching books about the topic. Surprisingly, the books I found repeatedly were books that talked about rebuilding credit, working on your credit, repairing your credit, boosting credit score, and so on. None talked about how to start building credit.

I figured I'd ask the people I know with the most credit history and experience—my parents. I reached out to them and asked how to start building my credit. After they agreed I should open an account, we talked about what to do. They suggested I go to the credit and savings cooperative and take out a loan, pay the loan in full, and then apply for a credit card. Then, I should have some credit history on my report.

I was okay with that, but it didn't make sense to me why they told me that now. That would've been helpful two years ago to have some history now. But they didn't tell me sooner because I didn't ask and it didn't occur to them.

A negative culture and misconception surrounds credit cards, mainly that they keep people in debt. We read stories all the time of how in debt people are or how much they pay in fees. No wonder there is this feeling of banks wanting all your money. Now I understand why my parents didn't teach me about credit. Credit is portrayed as a bad thing instead of being a tool for helping an individual. Credit helps you get better loans and better interest for purchases. Plus, you get rewards for using it. There's nothing bad about that! Credit, by itself, is a tool everyone can use to further their personal finance growth. Instead of saving for ten years to buy a home, you can save for one year and use credit to buy it. You can use it to purchase tools that will help you personally, like a car to commute to work. The same is true for credit cards, which are an extension of your credit and its physical representation. Use them to buy the tools that will help you expand your business or use them daily to benefit from the cashback. When your credit cards get lost or stolen, you can call the bank and they will help you out. When your cash gets lost or stolen, who do you call? *En fin*. Credit and credit cards have no downside when used correctly. They are amazing personal growth tools.

I'm sure you are reading this because you want to know what credit and credit history is, to build credit, or to simply understand how it works. As I write this book, I am sharing with you my credit journey, from having zero experience in credit and nonexistent credit history to having a number of cards and an excellent credit score. Throughout the book, I'll share my experience, dos and don'ts, and a couple of tricks and input from people you could call experts on the matter. I want to make sure you understand one thing: Yes, this is a game, these are the rules, and here's how to play it.

To read more about common myths and misconceptions surrounding credit, visit me at LuccianoDiazSkoff.com and reach out on Instagram @LuccianoDiazSkoff.

CHAPTER 3

What the F%*#
Is Credit?

---

*"The best way to deal with credit card
debt is to educate yourself."*

—MARK ROSEN

What is this thing that people are always talking about but you don't see? Some people have it; some don't. Others have had bad experiences with it, while the rest just boast how much of it they have. You know that you can buy things with it, even though you do not have cash. Well, it's precisely that, "the ability of a customer to obtain goods or services before payment, based on the trust that payment will be made in the future."[6] You see,

---

6   "Credit: Definition of Credit by Oxford Dictionary on Lexico.com Also Meaning of Credit," Lexico Dictionaries | English. Lexico Dictionaries.

it doesn't matter what you buy, or where, or how much, or how many times you purchase it. None of that matters as long as you pay it in the end. That trust will allow you to buy more things and is the basis of understanding on which the financial world runs.

Now, you might think that credit is strictly used for credit cards. You are wrong. That's one of the tools you need to have access to it. Credit cards are part of revolving credit: With it, you are given a maximum borrowing limit. You can make charges up to that limit as well as make a minimum payment each month. Alternatively, the amount you pay can be any portion of your outstanding charges up to the full amount. If you make a partial payment, you will carry forward the remainder of your balance or revolve the debt. Most credit cards count as revolving credit. This means that they are the type of loan that does not have a fixed number of payments, which is an installment loan. Revolving credit lets you access money from an account with a set amount of money, called your credit limit. You can only access up to that amount. As you start paying the account, you regain the ability to keep borrowing money from that account, thus allowing you to keep using the money available to you.

Just so you have an idea, out of the 253 million adults in the US, 20.2 million have a personal loan.[7] By 2017, 108.66 million Americans had an auto loan[8] and 62.9 percent, or almost one hundred sixty million Americans had a

---

7   Elyssa Kirkham, "Personal Loan Statistics," LendingTree, January 24, 2020.

8   "35 Essential Auto Loan Statistics (2020 Update)," PolicyAdvice, December 7, 2020.

home equity line of credit.[9] Do you know how many people have at least one credit card? Seven out of ten people have them. That's over 191 million Americans who either have a credit card, a charge card, or both.[10] That is insane! What is also scary is 47 percent of cardholders in 2020 carry a balance. In other words, they have credit card debt. The worst part is that the balance is not one they carry for a couple of months, they carry it for a couple of years! I'm baffled to know that people misuse the most accessible and easiest tool available to build credit. And no, this revolving credit debt is not from an auto loan or mortgage, but directly from the credit cards of people who live beyond their means. Yes, there are instances you need to use them, for example, a pandemic. This year, 34 percent of millennials added debt to their existing card debt due to the health crisis.[11]

One night after a family dinner, I was watching TV with my mom. A commercial from Credit Karma played, and she asked, "Does that work?" "What do you mean?" I asked. "Well, I want to get another card. Actually, I would like to have an American Express again." It felt great to finally hear my mother say she wants a card and asked me how to do it. My heart skipped a beat from the excitement. I told her what Credit Karma was, how it worked, and that she could monitor her credit from there. She got excited too because she was learning something new.

9   Michael Neal, "Mortgage Debt Has Peaked. Why Has the Share of Homeowners with a Mortgage Fallen to a 13-Year Low?" Urban Institute, August 20, 2019.

10   Jamie Gonzalez-Garcia and Allie Johnson, "Credit Card Ownership Statistics," CreditCards.com, January 15, 2020.

11   AJ Horch, "Almost Half of America Is Now Carrying Credit Card Debt, and More of It," CNBC, May 4, 2020.

After explaining how to monitor her credit, she told me the reason why she wanted an Amex card.

Times were hard when my brother and I were young. It was even harder for an immigrant father, constantly being passed over for promotions and bigger projects. I still feel that to this day. My parents were not making enough money to keep the family afloat. While my mom could not leave her job, my dad had no other choice. He started his own business to support the family. My mother's credit card played a key role. Not only was she able to provide for the family, but my dad was also able to jumpstart the business. That American Express credit card kept them from going bankrupt, losing the cars, and losing the house. My mom racked up $10,000 in debt, which she eventually paid, but had to close the card to stop the spending.

Since then, she has not had another Amex card until now.

Once we finished the conversation, she told me, "I'm sorry for closing the card, now I know it was bad for my credit." I told her, "That is not the point. You used the credit card as intended. It saved you. It saved us. That card did more for you than cash could ever have done."

That is exactly what I want you to know. Even though this book is about opening, keeping, and maintaining credit cards, life happens. My parents were able to start again thanks to that credit card. They used the money available to them. She closed the card with debt, money she couldn't have otherwise used if not for credit.

LET'S CONTINUE WITH THE TYPES OF CREDIT

Installment credit, on the other hand, is a loan for a specific sum of money, plus interest and fees, you agree to repay in a series of equal monthly payments (installments) over a set period. Student loans, car loans, and mortgages are all examples of installment credit.

Charge cards, once commonly issued by retailers to use exclusively in their establishment, are relatively rare these days. Charge cards are used in much the same way as credit cards, but they don't permit you to carry a balance: You must pay all charges in full every month. Those banks that do let you "pay over time" come with a hefty fee.

Next, service credit consists of your contracts with service providers, such as gas and electric utilities, cable and internet providers, cellular phone companies, and gyms. These companies provide their services to you each month with the understanding that you will pay for them after the fact.

Modern credit scoring systems, including the most recent versions of the FICO Score and VantageScore, can factor your service payment history into your credit scores. Still, those payments are not always reported to the credit bureaus. Some programs enable you to share utility and cell phone payment records to be considered in credit scores based on Experian data. Yes, I know, you've probably been using credit without knowing what it was. It's a fantastic tool that, if used right, will open a world of possibilities of what you can do with money.

While you might think that credit is something new within the last fifty years, it actually predates the use of coins and currency in the world. Take the Euro for example, which is only twenty-one years old, or the US dollar, which is 170 years old. Let's consider the oldest currency still in use in the world, the pound/sterling/ sterling pound, at 1,200 years old, or even the oldest coin used, the Lydian coin from 2,600 years ago. Yet credit has been around for more than 5,000 years. Let's go down history road for a minute.

Americans now have over $12.4 trillion borrowed through mortgages, credit cards, student loans, auto loans, and other types of credit. How did we get here? It starts with the Sumerians. It is thought that around 3,500 B.C., consumer loans appeared to be used for agricultural purposes. About 89 percent of the population of Sumer lived in cities, thus being the first urban civilization. To feed all those people living in the city, they needed to harvest more crops. To do that, they needed land. To access even more land while being short on capital, credit became the tool that fed the people.

Fast forward to 1,800 B.C., the Code of Hammurabi depicts the first law of credit, capping the interest on grain loans (33 percent) and silver loans (20 percent). The first-ever millionaire real estate transaction recorded in history of someone buying land with credit was in 50 B.C. Rome, where Cicero writes about how his neighbor bought six hundred twenty-five acres of land for 11.5 million sesterces: *"nomina facit, negotium conficit"*—or, "he uses credit to complete the purchase."

While the Roman Empire used credit to continue its expansion, inflation and long-term economic decline got the best of them. So much so that its effects were still being felt around Europe four hundred years after its fall. Sometime during the Dark Ages in Europe, the church banned the practice of charging interest on loans. Economic activity during this period ground to a halt.

It was not until the age of discovery that credit picked up again. In the 1500s, explorers and merchants began missions to faraway lands, increasing the demand for new capital and credit. While the trips were being financed by the state, one particular country standardized the business. England, under Henry VIII, became the first country to establish a legal rate of interest of 10 percent in 1545. Anything higher was considered usury. It was not until 1787 that philosopher Jeremy Bentham wrote a treatise called, "A Defense of Usury." He argued that restrictions on interest rates harmed the ability to raise capital for innovation. If risky, new ventures couldn't be funded, growth became limited.

Although creditors kept a record of who owed them money, they did not share that information. The earliest available account of credit reporting, similar to what we have today, originated in the nineteenth century. English tailors would swap information on customers who failed to pay their debts. This system of keeping and sharing tabs on who has a debt with who is the birth of modern consumer credit. Apparently, people in those days failed to pay their debts too. That is why, in 1826 England, the Manchester Guardian Society was formed and began issuing a monthly newsletter with information about those people.

Some fifteen years later in 1841 in New York, the Mercantile Agency was founded with the same purpose as the Guardian Society. In this case, they had a network of correspondents systemizing rumors about debtors' assets with a massive lender. On the eve of the Civil War, the Mercantile Agency is renamed the R. G. Dun & Company. By 1864, they finalized an alphanumeric system for tracking companies' creditworthiness that would remain in use until the twentieth century.

That system changed in 1899 with the foundation of the oldest of the three major credit agencies in the United States. The Retail Credit Company in Atlanta began compiling an extensive list of creditworthy customers throughout the nation. The company would later change its name to Equifax.

Entering the twentieth century, we saw the revolutionary Model T car from Henry Ford, designed for the "great multitude" of people to access. Sadly, it was not affordable for most families since they had to pay in cash. In 1919, General Motors (GM) solved that problem by loaning consumers the money they needed to buy a new car. The General Motors Acceptance Corporation (GMAC) was founded and popularized the idea of installment plan financing. Consumers could now get a new car with just a 35 percent down payment at the time of financing.

Ford's new manufacturing technique of mass production and assembly lines revolutionized the industry. Efficient US factories were pumping out cheaper consumer products and appliances by 1930. Installment loans and credit in the hands of consumers made goods more accessible. Washing machines, furniture, refrigerators, phonographs, and radios could now be bought on installment plans. Credit was so big and revolutionary in this period that two-thirds of all autos were bought on installment plans.

With so much credit and loans going around the United States, new opportunities arose. By 1950, typical middle-class Americans already had revolving credit accounts at different merchants. At the same time, Diners Club introduced its charge card, which helped open the floodgates for other consumer credit products. With so many loans and accounts, who was keeping track?

Welcome big data. Early credit reporters used millions of index cards, sorted in a massive filing system, to track consumers around the country. To get the latest information, agencies would scour local newspapers to notice arrests, promotions, marriages, and deaths, attaching this information to individual credit files. A lot has changed since then.

Thanks to the Diners Club pioneering in the charge card space, competitors saw a huge opportunity. In 1958, BankAmericard, now Visa, "dropped" in Fresno, California. American Express and Mastercard soon followed, offering Americans general credit for a wide range of purchases. Now, even more Americans had access to revolving credit accounts. In 1960, American credit bureaus issued sixty million credit reports. That was a third of the American population at the time.

All those credit reports were kept on paper registries. Can you imagine the amount of work to keep sixty million reports up to date on paper? That is why, in 1964, the Association of Credit Bureaus in the US started to study the implementation of computer technologies to standardize credit reporting. But it wasn't until 1970 that the first Fair Credit Reporting Act was passed, establishing a legal standard for reporting agencies. This is when we started to see the first version of what our current model looks like.

Sometime around the 1980s, the three major credit bureaus, Equifax, Experian, and TransUnion, were able to cover the country with their credit services. Although they did not use the FICO score to extend credit, they used a more subjective method: character. Yes, you read that right. Before the Fair, Isaac, and Company, what we know as FICO, promoted their credit model in 1989, lenders would decide to extend you credit on whether they liked you or not. Thankfully, that has changed.

All three credit bureaus adopted the FICO scoring model by 1991, revolutionizing the way lenders and businesses assessed consumer risk. It wasn't until 2006 that the only scoring model was challenged when the three largest credit bureaus created VantageScore. Even though FICO was still used in 90 percent of the market with VantageScore used in the other 10 percent, the latter was used to some capacity by 60 percent of financial institutions in 2019.

Thanks to the information age, the credit landscape has broadened. Now, any established business can partner up with a bank or financial institution and issue a credit card. Almost every financial decision you make affects your credit score and how the bank sees you. This new era of consumer credit helps better determine when you will default on a payment or how many days late you will pay. Banks pull your credit report to learn about you and assess their risk. Your credit report is used to make housing, employment, and insurance decisions.[12]

---

12   "Using Consumer Reports for Credit Decisions: What to Know

Like Suze Orman says, "Your credit score affects the interest rates you're offered on credit cards and loans, can be used to vet your job application, and in some states may influence your insurance premiums."[13]

Nowadays, consumers can monitor their information and credit reports easier than ever. Technology has allowed users to access their data from anywhere, anytime. This same technology has helped improve the predictive patterns of consumers and allowed consumers to learn more about credit. Banks can now reach new customers faster, providing a new way of accessing capital.[14]

A longtime friend and business owner, Fernando Mercado, has benefited from applying for credit cards online.

"Overcoming the unjustified fear that people have about credit and its use has opened doors for me to access capital. Credit is an important and vital tool for an ongoing business. It is sad that in Puerto Rico, access to credit is so difficult for businesspeople, but the internet opens the door to global alternatives."

Technology has permeated almost every part of our lives. Phones and apps are constantly gathering our ever-increasing data to enhance our experience. All this data is poised to change the credit landscape sooner rather than later, starting with the borrower's profile. Creditors will soon have a full view of who you are, and you are more than your credit score. This is supported by the new use

---

About Adverse Action and Risk-Based Pricing Notices," Federal Trade Commission, July 16, 2020.

13   Suze Orman, "Suze Orman's (Ridiculously Easy) Financial To-Do List," January 2010.

14   Jeff Desjardins, "The History of Consumer Credit in One Giant Infographic," *Visual Capitalist*, August 29, 2017.

of big data, machine learning, and deep learning, among other things.

In fact, "90 percent of the data in the world today has been created in the last two years."[15] By democratizing data and making it accessible to consumers, new players as well as new models are bringing innovating tech to the field. Neural networks and blockchain paired with advanced biometrics are constantly increasing the protection of a person's data and identity. This opens the door for new credit trends like alternative credit scoring, peer-to-peer lending, and micro-lending. You can also expect companies to fill the gap in new niche credit services. The future of credit will be exciting!

THE CREDIT YOU CAME HERE FOR

That was a summary of how credit started and how it has evolved through time. But let's get to what you are here for: credit cards. The Diners Club, mentioned in the timeline, is how the charge card became the credit card we now know. This Diners Club card is the world's first multipurpose charge card. A businessman named Frank McNamara was having dinner in New York when he noticed he didn't have his wallet in the jacket he brought, and he needed to pay the tab. That sparked the idea of a card that holds you accountable.

It started as a membership service in hotels and restaurants. Around that time, individual stores would extend credit to their customers, allow them to run up a tab, and let them pay it later only if the owner knew they

15 "90% Of Global Data Was Created in the Last 2 Years—IBM," Optigra, November 6, 2014.

were good for the money. What the Diners Club did was provide its members with the benefit of credit in multiple locations. Used mainly for travel and entertainment, the Diners Club card claims the first credit card's title in widespread use. Although its purchases were made on credit, Diners Club was technically a charge card, meaning the bill had to be paid in full at the end of each month. By 1951, Diners Club had twenty thousand cardholders.[16]

But the charge card was invented five years earlier. Bank-issued charge cards originated in 1946 when a Brooklyn banker named John Biggins launched the Charg-It card. Charg-It purchases were forwarded to Biggins's bank. This middleman reimbursed the merchant and obtained payment from the customer in what came to be known as the "closed-loop" system. Purchases could only be made locally, and only bank customers could get a Charg-It card. Five years later, New York's Franklin National Bank followed suit, issuing its first charge card to its loan customers. With postwar America on the go, two dining and entertainment charge cards quickly followed. The first one, as we already talked about, was the Diners Club card. And the second one has been dominating since its debut: American Express.

American Express (Amex) is considered part of the Big Four credit cards, which set the stage for new cards and banks alongside Visa, Mastercard, and Discover.

The American Express card, which launched in 1958, had an altogether different provenance. Formed in 1850 as a competitor to the US Postal Service, American Express had introduced money orders in 1882, invented traveler's

---

16 Jay MacDonald and Taylor Tompkins, "The History of Credit Cards (Timeline & Major Events)," CreditCards.com, July 11, 2017.

checks in 1891, and contemplated a travel charge card as early as 1946, before Diners Club beat it to the punch.

American Express would soon claim its milestones by expanding its reach to other countries and introducing the first plastic card in 1959, replacing cardboard and celluloid. Within five years, one million American Express cards were in use at eighty-five thousand merchants, foreign and domestic. They also introduced the first metal card in 1999, the titanium Centurion Card, commonly known as the "Black Card." Elvis Presley was one of the earliest American Express card members.

At the same time, in 1958, Bank of America issued the BankAmericard—the first actual credit card to California customers. While the original Diners Club card required payment in full at the end of each month, BankAmericard users could pay off purchases over time. In 1976, BankAmericard became Visa. Visa is pronounced the same in every language—ideal for now a global corporation.

BankAmericard got a run for its money when a group of banks joined forces in 1966 to create the Interbank Card Association (ICA). In 1969, ICA started Master Charge: the Interbank Card, which became Mastercard, in 1979. Mastercard was the first payment card issued in the People's Republic of China.[17]

Discover is the newest major credit card network on the scene. Sears launched the Discover card in 1986, distinguishing it from the pack by charging no annual fees (AF) and offering higher credit limits than other cards at the

---

17   "Brand History," Mastercard Brand History, Logo Evolution, accessed December 30, 2020.

time. Discover was also the innovator of cash rewards on credit card purchases. At that time, Discover cardholders could earn rewards of up to 1 percent cashback on all purchases. Discover Financial Services purchased Diners Club International in 2008.[18]

CREDIT IN THE NEW ERA

Discover pioneered cash rewards, allowing cardholders to get a percentage back on purchases charged. And in 1989, Citibank made a deal with American Airlines to give consumers reward points to use for future flights. Today, consumers continue to use credit card rewards programs to earn cash or points for future purchases, including travel. In fact, more than 80 percent of credit card users have rewards programs associated with their cards.[19]

Two things have helped the widespread use of credit cards in the states. In the early decades, restrictive interstate banking laws curbed credit. But credit's big breakthrough came in 1978 when the Supreme Court ruled to allow nationally chartered banks to charge out-of-state customers the interest rate set in the bank's home state. Credit expanded as a result, and today the average American credit card holder has nearly four cards.[20]

The second move was on the part of the credit card companies. While they made money by charging stores

18 Sienna Kossman, "The History of Credit Cards: Ancient Times to Present Day," *The Balance*, August 8, 2019.

19 SoFi, "A History of Credit (and How to Manage Yours Better)," SoFi, February 3, 2017.

20 "The Consumer Credit Card Market," Consumerfinance.gov, December 2015.

transaction fees and charging interest on the debt, many credit card companies eliminated annual fees to stay competitive. Now, most credit cards do not have an annual fee. And those who have it cater to those who will take full advantage of their extra benefits (more on that in a later chapter).

To summarize, credit is not new. It has been used for the past five thousand years in many ways. What is new is its representation and what we can do with it. Instead of having to withdraw money from the bank, we can access it with a card from anywhere. Now, we can buy anything with credit, from a stove to a painting, a house, and beyond. And all those purchases give you something in return: cash, points, or miles.

Credit will continue to evolve as it has done through the years. As we produce more data, we will have more control of our credit. This accessibility to credit brings forth the most important goal for the future of credit: Through education and financial literacy, more people will be able to access it.

To discover what new tools are being developed in the credit world, visit me at LuccianoDiazSkoff.com and reach out on Instagram @LuccianoDiazSkoff.

CHAPTER 4.

~~Their~~ Rules. Your Game.

———

*"Learn the rules like a pro, so you
can break them like an artist."*

—PABLO PICASSO

Since you're now aware of credit and how it evolved into what we use today as credit cards, let me share how the game is played. Before jumping into it, there are three cardinal rules. Indisputably, you-cannot-have-credit-cards-if-you-cannot-follow-these rules: 1) Make sure that you have the cash when paying with your credit card. 2) Always, pay your debt, no matter what. In other words, never, never, never carry a balance. 3) Always pay in full and on time. Period. I want you to memorize these rules, learn them, know them as if they were part of you from the day you were born. Because if you don't, you will end up in debt.

You might miss a payment and think, "It's okay. It won't matter that much." Newsflash, it does. I can help you get the mark removed in another chapter. Or maybe you will carry a balance and pay the minimum and a little extra on the payment, then you will think, "It will not affect me that much." Sad news for you, you will have less money in your credit line. And that is not the point of having credit. You want all the money possible available to you, at your disposal, so you can use it when you need it.

Things happen in life, things like earthquakes, hurricanes, and pandemics, among many others. I experienced all three in Puerto Rico in less than three years. You may get laid off, go through a divorce, be in a car crash, or something much more horrible. Life comes out of nowhere and wallops you. Do not worry; credit is there for you. How? You will, at some point in your life, be strapped for cash. You can use credit to help yourself get out of your position and move to a better place. This is an exception to the rules. In this case, you need money to survive and should instead use the funds available in the future and leave the cash in your pocket.

Why should I insist on you following these rules? Because they will help you keep yourself in check. You won't have to worry ever again about the APR or interest rates on your credit cards. Interest rates are the rate at which a balance incurs interest charges. On the other hand, the annual percentage rate, or APR, is the interest rate plus any fees. This distinction differs only when it comes to loans. When it comes to credit cards, you can use them interchangeably. These rules will help you achieve that credit score that will give you access to the best rates, offers, and sign-up bonuses in the market.

Now, usually, a bank is the entity that will lend you the money for your loan. Before they do that, they need to know that you have money to pay them back. So, they will ask you for a document that proves you are employed. In other words, they want to ensure you are making money. They just can't give you the money without remotely knowing you will pay them back. You have the money the bank gave you; they know you can pay them back. What happens in the first month of using the loan? The bank checks how much of it you used and if you paid back what you used. They then send the information to an external entity (credit bureaus), and using a couple of other factors, they give you a score—a credit score. This score is used by other credit organizations to measure how good a borrower you are (i.e., demonstrating to lenders if you are a risky borrower or an exceptional one) and determine how much money they will let you borrow.

This credit score is based on a couple of factors that also build your credit report. Banks also look at your credit report to make a decision. Like previously mentioned, your credit report is your financial resume.

Of course, a bank or credit entity will not always let you borrow and go into debt if you're already heavily in debt or your income is insufficient to make debt payments. The credit issuers will not let you borrow money. Other reasons could include you don't have sufficient disposable income after you pay existing debt obligations. Your debt obligations represent a high percentage of your monthly income (for example, your unsecured debt obligations, such as loans not backed by collateral, are 50 percent or more of your total revenue). In other words, your disposable income is how much money you have left after you subtract your taxes, credit card debts, and other debts (debt obligations) from your total income. Another reason might be if they notice you have fully utilized all of your credit card lines in the last three months and have recently opened a significant amount of new credit accounts.[21]

Going back to your credit score: The entity that rates your credit and gives you a credit score is called FICO. Some people call your credit score a FICO score. Why? Because they are a significant analytics software company that provides products and services to both businesses and consumers. The Fair Isaac Corporation, originally known as the Fair, Isaac, and Company, changed its name to FICO in 2009 and is best known for producing the most widely used consumer credit scores that financial institutions use in deciding whether to lend money or issue credit. But they are not the only ones. Equifax, Experian, and Transunion also have their score system in the US. Unlike Fico, the rest are credit bureaus, or credit reporting agencies (CRA), which banks and credit entities report to. On top of each of the credit bureaus having their scoring system, Equifax, Experian, and Transunion partnered up and developed VantageScore to rival FICO.

These two are the most used credit scoring models, and by that I mean they have software that can analyze a credit report to generate a credit score. Remember, their goal is to predict the likelihood that a person will fall at least ninety days behind on a bill within the next twenty-four months. Lenders also use the other three national credit bureaus credit scoring to have a complete profile before making a decision. The scores you see for free

---

21   "How Your Apple Card Application Is Evaluated," Apple Support, June 29, 2020.

in an app or on a website are often called educational scores. They simply provide you an overview of your credit history. You can use it to check for errors in your report or have an idea where your credit score stands.

I urge you to check at least your FICO and VantageScore before deciding on a new card. Even though their scoring system varies, you will have an excellent idea of your credit score. To have a more accurate credit score, I use the myFICO website. It costs $40 every month, but then you will have your complete credit score and report at your convenience.

Since we are talking about FICO, 90 percent of lenders use your FICO score to make a decision.[22] How do they figure your score? The categories are payment history and derogatory marks, utilization rate, age of credit, total accounts, and credit inquires.[23]

Let me go one by one on their weight and impact on your credit score.

"You don't have to use a credit card a lot to build your credit score—you just have to pay your credit card bills on time and pay those cards off in full every month."

—DAVID BACH

22 "Credit Checks: What Are Credit Inquiries and How Do They Affect Your FICO Score?" myFICO, accessed October 9, 2020.

23 "How Are FICO Scores Calculated?" myFICO, November 19, 2019.

PAYMENT HISTORY

Starting with your history, payment history and deroga-tory marks count for 35 percent of your credit score.[24] Why? Well, you must show you are a responsible person who pays on time. Because if you do not pay on time, you get a mark that lasts in your history for seven years. You do not want that. In other words, payment history shows your track of paying your credit accounts on time. And this is for every line of credit you have. The report shows if you are thirty, sixty, ninety, one hundred twenty, or more days late. So, always pay your bills.

Let me show you what happens if you miss a payment and how that one missed payment affects your credit nega-tively. Let's say you got yourself a brand-new card with a couple of perks here and there, and you've been pay-ing it, the total balance, on time, every month for eleven months, right? Now, on your twelfth month, something happened and you didn't pay your card. You think, "Oh well, it's my first time. I don't think that matters a lot." Out of the twelve months you've been using your card, you missed a payment, or you've paid eleven out of twelve months. That is 92 percent of your payment history. In other words, 92 percent of the time, you'll pay on time. Not bad. But you just bumped yourself down to the "infe-rior" category on a high impact category that can make it very difficult to establish your credit.

A colleague and very good friend of mine, Leandro Diaz, had his credit suffer from a single missed payment. One day while eating lunch, he asked, "Lucciano, can you see

---

24 "How Payment History Impacts Your Credit Score," myFICO, accessed December 30, 2020.

what is happening with my credit? I've been trying to pre-qualify for an Amex, but no offers show up. Why do you think that is?" After a quick look at his Credit Karma, we found it. Last year, he had missed a payment that lowered his credit score by about thirty-five points. He has still seen the effect almost a year later. Although he had managed to get back on track paying his cards, that single missed payment has kept his credit score under seven hundred.

Twelve months passed, and you didn't miss a payment. But your report says that in twenty-four months, you paid, on time, twenty-three months, or 96 percent of the time. Plus, you still have a derogatory mark for not paying on time for another six years. Hey, some news for you: You are still in the "very poor" category of this high impact category. Why high impact? Remember, it is 35 percent of your credit score. Why very poor? Because if you have less than 97 percent, you're in the "poor" category; 98 percent, "fair"; 99 percent, "good"; and 100 percent means you have always paid on time, which is the "excellent" category. So, don't be fooled that one missed payment doesn't affect you that much.

Now, let's say you have five cards instead of one. This is a little more forgiving because instead of having one missed payment in twelve months (eleven out of twelve, or 92 percent), you would have one missed payment in sixty months (sixty possible payments), or fifty-nine out of sixty, which is 98 percent. You'd be in the appropriate category. This is the importance of having more than one card. Let me tell you how this works. Every month, for every card, is an opportunity to pay on time, yes? In a year, you have twelve months of possible payments, per card. Now, you have five cards. In a year, you have sixty months of potential on-time payments. Now, you are getting how having more cards works in your favor, right? Out of those sixty possible payments, you paid sixty months on time, or one hundred percent payment history.

Let's go back to the previous example. Missing a payment in one year with one card has a more significant toll on your credit score if you miss a payment in a year with five cards. This will help you understand the category: a total of on-time payments divided by the sum of possible payments.

And that derogatory mark? If you have only one, you can send a letter to the credit bureau or the agency that extended you the credit, telling them why you missed the payment and that it won't happen again. And most of the time, they'll take it off your report once they receive the payment. Derogatory marks include late payments and collection accounts for charged-off loans and lines of credit or unpaid medical bills. That is not all: Public records like unpaid child support, unpaid alimony, delinquent taxes, foreclosures, and auto repossessions all add marks to your credit report. The worst of the derogatory marks is bankruptcy, the most detrimental of all marks. We will go further into this in Chapters 7, 1, and 13.

Be careful, because only one derogatory mark puts you in the "fair" category in this segment. That, paired with the payment history, makes up 35 percent of your credit history. Zero derogatory marks are "excellent." Two to three derogatory marks are "poor." Four or more, you end up in the "very poor" category.

Again, please, always pay on time. Autopay is a great way not to miss a payment, or you can set a calendar reminder to always remember.

If you doubt how your payment history is calculated, just use this formula: your on-time payments divided by your total payments.

CREDIT CARD UTILIZATION RATE

The second category, and the second heaviest, is credit card utilization rate. This has a 30 percent impact on your credit score and is the one that most people are not conscious of.[25] Remember, if you follow the rules, you'll never have to worry about any of the categories. Credit card utilization rate means how much of your credit you have used. All of your cards have a credit limit, and their sum is the total credit available to you.

Let's say you have one card with a $100 credit limit on it. Since it's your only card, you have $100 available to you, of which you use $10. Utilization rate is total credit balance divided by total credit card limits. When your statement comes to pay the bill, it will show that you have used 10 percent of your credit. Not bad, right? That's not a lot, but it puts you in the good range. You want to be in the excellent range. That way, you'll have a

25 "How Owing Money Can Impact Your Credit Score," myFICO, accessed December 30, 2020.

higher credit score and can access better deals. Ideally, you want to have a 0 percent credit card utilization rate, or between 0 percent and 9 percent.

But... that's counterintuitive! You take out a credit card to use money not yet available to you. So why is using it bad? Because banks want to know that you are not a risky borrower. Here's how to work around that credit utilization rate not affecting you and avoid having to worry about it. First, **do not wait for your statement to come**. It makes sense to use your credit card at the start of the cycle and wait to pay it off at the end of it because you only pay interest after the payment due date.

The payment due date is the date set by the bank (around 28 days) after your statement bill closes. In other words, the bank gives you a set amount of time after the end of the cycle to pay your bill without interest. In the statement, you will see the payment date, the minimum payment, and the interest to be accrued if not paid by the set date. Some banks give you the option to pay more than the minimum to avoid interest.

That is what credit is for, right? But by that time, the bank has pulled the information on your credit account(s) and knows how much of it you have used. Before that happens, get into the habit of paying off your cards two to three days after using them, every few days, or, if that is not possible, pay the total amount before the bill comes. The idea here is that by the time your cycle ends and you get your bank statement in the mail, you already paid your balance. Ergo, you have a 0 percent utilization rate and are staying in that excellent range.

Second, your goal here is to increase your credit score drastically. Your score is inversely proportional to your credit card utilization rate. The higher the rate, the lower your score; it's that simple. Let us use the same $100 from the last example. Now you use $90 from that card. That is a 90 percent utilization rate! But that won't matter if **you pay your balance in full** before the cycle ends.

I wanted to know how my credit would be affected if I carried a balance. So, I did a little experiment. I used 10 percent of my credit and did not pay until after the bank reported my utilization rate. What happened next? Twenty-three points. Yes, Michael Jordan's number. But my credit lowered by twenty-three points for just carrying 10 percent of my credit limit. Imagine how much higher your credit score could be if you simply lower your utilization rate.

That was the only time I let myself carry a balance with the sole purpose of research. I am honestly the worst customer for any credit card company out there. I always pay off my balance, in full, on time, every time. I never carry a balance. You do not want to carry a balance on your cards or affect your credit score. If you find yourself maintaining a balance often, you should sit down and analyze your expenses to see what you can cut back on.

Third, **get more cards**! Really! This will help in three ways: showing the total accounts open, lowering your utilization rate, and, if you're smart about choosing cards, enjoying the perks. I'll talk more about total open accounts later in this chapter.

How can having more credit cards help lower your utilization rate? Instead of using $90 out of a single card with a $100 credit limit and having a 90 percent utilization rate, if you have four more cards with a $200 credit limit for a total of $900 and spend the same $90, your utilization rate lowers to 10 percent! And you go from being in the poor range to being in the good range, thus increasing your credit score.

Since now you have more cards, and assuming you were smart about the cards you chose, I'll teach you what you need to look for. You probably have perks for airport lounges, extra cashback, or points you can redeem for anything else, even free flights. That's great! Keep in mind that you should always keep your utilization rate at 0 percent, or at least between 0 percent and 9 percent, which is the excellent range. If you go above and land in the 10 percent to 29 percent, you are considered in the good range. Fair is when you use between 30 percent to 49 percent. Poor is from 50 percent to 74 percent. And very poor is 75 percent and up.

If you are not sure how credit card utilization rate is calculated, use this formula: total credit card balances divided by your total credit card limits.

In the process of writing this book, conversations about money became frequent in my household, something that hadn't happen before. My mom, my dad, and my brother now openly talk about credit card perks and when to use and pay their balances. One night, my mom asked me how she could get a perfect credit score. (I smiled; I've been waiting for this moment.) I sat down with my mom, opened an account in Credit Karma, and saw two things. First, she had a healthy seven hundred forty-five credit score. The second thing, she had a 40 percent utilization rate. She has never missed a payment, never gone bankrupt, and never had an account go to collections. I told my mom, "Your report looks great. You just have to work on lowering your utilization rate."

And she did just that. After going over how credit works, she lowered her utilization rate to 10 percent in a couple of months. I will forever cherish her reaction when she opened the app and saw her credit jump eighty-four points to the eight hundred credit score range. It was the best day of the year.

We have covered what makes up 65 percent of your credit score. As you can see, credit is a simple numbers game. And trust me, it really is simple. Do not be scared. This does not involve any complex operations or any of that crazy stuff they teach engineers (trust me, I'm one). You can figure out what to do, when to do it, how much to spend, and even when to apply for your next card with basic adding, subtracting, and dividing. The thing that matters the most in this game is time. I'm sure you've heard the saying, The best time to plant a tree (or the best time to invest) was ten years ago. The second-best time is now. The same thing goes for credit.

The most influential factor toward your credit score, and your best ally, is time. The longer the time you hold onto an active credit card the longer your payment history, and the older your credit history is the more you solidify your credit score to the extent that missing a payment (do not recommend), closing accounts (depending on which one), and opening new accounts (depends on the timing) will not have a significant impact on your credit score. Start building your credit now.

One last thing: You might hear that using less than 30 percent of your credit limit is healthy and that you should carry a balance to "show the banks you are using your card." I differ. What does utilization rate mean? You carry a balance. What happens when you carry a balance? Interest kicks in. How do banks make money? By charging you interest fees when carrying a balance. That is the banks' business model and how they operate.

Banks typically make money in three ways: net interest margin, or the spread between their earnings and paybacks on loans; interchange fees, or the fees a store has to pay the bank whenever you pay with the bank's card; and fees. The bank's biggest income is credit card interest fees. Take Capital One Bank, for example. By September 30 of 2017, their credit card interest fees income amounted to $10,700,548,000.[26] That's a whole lot of money coming just from fees.

Thus, save your money, keep your utilization rate low or close to 0 percent, and never carry a balance. And like Hill Harper says, "Credit card interest payments are the dumbest money of all." [27]

---

26   Joe Resendiz, "How Credit Card Companies Make and Earn Money," ValuePenguin, December 12, 2019.

27   Beth Pinsker, "A Doctor on TV, Hill Harper Is a Money Guru in Real Life," Reuters, May 13, 2019.

AGE OF CREDIT

The next category is pretty straight forward: the age of credit. Yes, the age of *your* credit. How old is your credit? That alone is 15 percent of your total credit score.[28] It may not seem like a lot, but it is the factor that will muscle up your credit score *and* your credit history in the long run. In this case, the relation between the age of credit and credit score is directly proportional. The longer you have credit, the better your score is. The FICO score in this category considers the following things: how long the oldest account has been open, the age of the newest account, and the overall average or the average age of open accounts.

You will typically see the length of credit (how long the oldest account has been open) and the overall average in your credit report and credit score apps. Aim for nine-plus years in the average age of accounts to score "excellent" in this category. Suppose someone has an average age of account of ten months, even though their oldest account is twelve months old. Since that person is still under two years in this category, they are in the very poor range. To get to the poor range, they would have to wait a year and some change to get there. This ranges from two to four years average credit age.

Currently, my oldest account is at ten months, with an average of seven months. In other words, I'm under two years in this category, which puts me in the very poor range. In two more years, I'll be in the two to four years, which is still poor. Once you get to the five to six years

---

28   "How the Length of Your Credit History Impacts Your FICO Score," myFICO, accessed December 30, 2020.

average age of credit, you are in the fair range. And from seven to eight years, you are good.

To calculate your credit's average age, use this formula: total months of opened accounts divided by the number of accounts.

That is why it is crucial to start building your credit as soon as you can. The more time you have borrowing money, the higher your credit score will be. The banks want to know how much experience you have borrowing and paying back money. The only way you can show that is with time. Heck, as I was writing this, I thought to myself: Where could my credit score have been if I had opened a card ten years ago when I was eighteen, or if my parents would have put me as an authorized user on one of their cards? The importance of time is invaluable.

Speaking of authorized users, here is something you can do right now. Some might call this a hack; others might view it as not worth it. Get yourself authorized to use a card, also known as piggybacking. The idea is not to use the card, but to pull that person's credit to your side. That is what my friend's parent did. When Christian Colón was fourteen years old, his dad added him as an authorized user. Now that he is in his thirties he has an age of credit of over forty years, longer than he has been alive.

It's true that as an authorized user, you do not build credit of your own if you use that card. On the other hand, being an authorized user increases your chances of getting approved. But soon, that won't be the case. In the next FICO model update, they will not take your authorized user's credit into consideration. And I understand why, because that is not your credit.

TOTAL ACCOUNTS

Total accounts are just 10 percent of your credit history.[29] Want to be "excellent" in this category? Have twenty-one open accounts. I know it sounds ridiculous, but that is what the current credit score model recommends. Do not worry too much about this category, and do not be confused by it. Most people think that a person with numerous credit cards is having money problems. That is not necessarily true for savvy individuals, and it is not how credit agencies view it.

Instead, they see how the more credit cards you have, the better you are at managing your money. To get to the good range in this category, you should have eleven or more credit products. Most of you will probably have more than eleven credit cards once you master the credit game.

How many cards is too many? It's not the number that you think. Walter Cavanagh of Santa Clara, California, has roughly 1,500 credit cards open in his name. That is around a $1.7 million line of credit.[30] Having ten, thirty, or fifty cards is no big deal compared to this guy.

---

29   "Types of Credit and How They Affect Your FICO Score," myFICO, accessed December 30, 2020.

30   Alexandra Mondalek, "Man Has Almost 1,500 Credit Cards and Near-Perfect Credit Score | Money," *Time*, January 4, 2016.

CREDIT INQUIRIES

Our last category is credit inquires. Don't get too worried by them since they are part of the process. Of course, we like to see our credit score report with everything green on it and a massive banner in all categories that says, "Excellent." Once you become an avid player of the credit card game, credit inquiries will not bother you much. Credit inquiries constitute the remaining 10 percent of your credit score.[31] Inquiries are commonly known as pulls, and there are two types: soft pulls and hard pulls.

Soft pulls pertain to when you rent a house or are pre-approved for a credit card. It's a simple credit check. On the other hand, hard pulls happen when you are going to accumulate debt, for example, buying a car or applying for a credit card. Hard pulls affect your credit and stay in your credit history for two years. The good thing is, over time, the impact on your credit reduces and when the inquiries drop off your credit score, you will see your score jump up a little bit.

Trick: Instead of applying for a credit card you do not know if you will be approved for and then having that inquiry in your credit history for two years, I recommend visiting the website of the institution offering the card and checking to see if you are pre-qualified. If you are, go ahead and apply. If you are not, save yourself from being denied and still getting the inquiry.

---

31 "How New Credit Impacts Your Credit Score," myFICO, accessed December 30, 2020.

When searching for pre-qualified cards, do not get it confused with pre-approval. A pre-approval is when the lender has already screened you to see if you meet the card requirements. They typically send the notification by mail. These days, you can find it in your lender's portal if you have an account. Meanwhile, a pre-qualification means searching for a card to see if you meet the requirements. I learned this the hard way because I did not have this information at hand. By the time I was approved for my first credit card, I already had eight hard inquiries in my credit history weighing down on my credit score.

***

I've laid out and explained the five things the current credit scoring platforms, FICO and Vantage Score, use to determine your credit score. Although they are not technically rules, they serve as guidelines for assessing and monitoring your credit's health. Once you start building credit, use credit apps to visually track your improvement. Most of them include a dashboard with each of these categories. The biggest takeaway here is the three rules to follow: If you do not have the cash, do not use your credit card. Always pay your debt, preferably before the statements come. And never carry a balance. Pay in full and on time.

Let me show you how these rules work together and how they tie in with the categories. By not having the cash at hand and using your credit, you run the risk of carrying a balance, having a utilization rate higher than 10 percent, and maybe missing a payment. Waiting to pay your balance after the cycle ends (statement comes in) means you have a utilization rate higher than 0 percent and might not have the money to pay the bill in full, which then leads you to carry a balance.

You might not be able to pay the bill at all because you were not tracking your spending (paying the balance every few days lets you know where you stand). On top of that, you get a derogatory mark. Carrying a balance causes you to pay interest on it. We do not want to give money to the bank other than what we used. Follow these three rules, and I guarantee you will be saved from all of this.

"If you don't take good care of your credit, then your credit won't take good care of you."[32]

The takeaway for this chapter is that your credit score is calculated using five categories: 1) payment history and derogatory marks; 2) utilization rate; 3) age of credit; 4) total accounts; and 5) credit inquires: thirty-five percent, 30 percent, 15 percent, 10 percent, and 10 percent, respectively.

Payment history and derogatory marks are 35 percent of your credit score. Every month you have an open credit card is a chance to pay your balance. Make sure you do not miss a payment. This will stay in your credit report for seven years as well as derogatory marks. Every late payment is a derogatory mark. Bankruptcy, an account in collections, court judgments, and other public records, like foreclosures, add to those marks. Avoid them at all costs.

Utilization rate is 30 percent of your credit score. Banks will say to use less than 30 percent of your total credit

---

32   "How to Improve Your Credit Score," eLoan, accessed September 18, 2020.

limit. Remember, this is how banks make money. The rule says to stay below 10 percent. I recommend just keeping it as low as possible, even at 0 percent.

Age of credit is 15 percent of your credit score. That is the amount of time the oldest account was opened. In this category, you and the banks will also see your average age of credit. Average age of credit is the total months of opened accounts divided by the number of accounts. Only time will help you with this.

Total accounts is 10 percent of your credit score. How many credit cards do you have? The more the merrier.

Credit inquiries is 10 percent of your credit score. Every time you apply for a credit card, whether you are approved or not, you get a hard inquiry, or "hard pull." This stays in your report for up to two years. Getting pre-approved or trying to see if you are pre-qualified is only a "soft pull" and does not show up.

To see how each of these categories affect your credit and calculate their impact, visit me at LuccianoDiazSkoff. com and reach out on Instagram @LuccianoDiazSkoff.

CHAPTER 5.

Your First Date

———

"The 85 Percent Solution: Getting started is more important than becoming an expert."

—RAMIT SETHI

Now that you know what credit is and how your credit score works, let's get you your first credit card. This might be a little bit confusing for some of you because of all the credit cards out there. Do not worry; the best card is the one available to you.

Hundreds of credit products offer the best cashback, the best lounge access at airports (that's right, a place just for cardholders to sit back and relax while you wait for your flight), or the most points toward something, but that comes later. What you want is to start building credit, the smart way, right now.

Your first card most probably will not have all the perks mentioned before nor a high credit limit. It will be a simple student's card or a credit builder card with just the right amount of credit at your disposal. Almost every bank, card issuer, or network has a credit starting card or a credit building card. Most of the time, they are the same thing—a tool to build your credit.

I want to distinguish between credit card networks and credit card issuers before you go out looking for your first card. Should this matter to you? Of course! "Finances are an important part of life, and the more you know about the products you use, the better off you'll be in the future," says Matt Freeman, head of credit card products at Navy Federal Credit Union.[33] A credit card issuer is a financial institution, for example Chase Bank, Citibank, and Bank of America, that gives you a credit card.

On the other hand, a credit card network is a company that provides a communication system between a merchant and an issuer to complete a credit card transaction. Examples of this are American Express, Discover, MasterCard, and Visa. In some cases, companies can be both credit card issuers and credit card networks (like American Express and Discover). Since American Express can issue its cards while providing communication between the merchant and the issuer, you'll never see a Visa or Mastercard logo on an American Express-issued credit card. When the printed card needs a network, for example, a Wells Fargo or Capital One credit card, you will most commonly find a Visa logo and the Mastercard logo, respectively.

There are many ways to start building credit. This next section will present the most commonly used methods of starting credit with credit cards. If you cannot take

---

33   John Egan, "Credit Card Companies: What You Should Know," Credit Karma, January 12, 2021.

this route, either because you do not have a friend or family member who could add you on their credit card as an authorized user or you simply do not want to handle credit cards, you have other options to start. Do not get me wrong; you can combine the credit cards with loans, which is, in my opinion, excellent. Along the way, you will add your first card to your credit mix and, hopefully, a mortgage.

One known but not spoken trick to fortifying your credit score is credit mix. Credit mix is the different types of credit in a consumer's credit report. This means that having other credit lines like student loans or automobile loans in your history will help your score. This shows the bank that you are a responsible borrower and can borrow money for different things, not just credit cards. This is hidden in the total accounts section of your credit score. This does not mean that you should go out and apply for credit cards and loans that you don't need to improve your credit score.

"You must gain control over your money or the lack of it will forever control you."

—DAVE RAMSEY[34]

Keep in mind that opening new accounts also affects other parts of your score, such as hard inquiries, total age of credit, whether you can pay it, your utilization rate and your balance, and ultimately your credit score. We must be smart about when to ask for another line of credit. But remember that this part is only 10 percent

34 Dave Ramsey and Sharon Ramsey, *Financial Peace Revisited* (New York: Viking, 2003). 20

of your credit score, so do not stress too much about it. With time, you'll have an excellent mark in this category.

The following options are not ordered in a specific way for you to go on one by one when trying to get a credit card. The goal here is to read every one of them, assess the situation you are in (maybe you are a student, got your first job, or want to start building credit), and then look at the suitable options and apply. Let's start.

Right off the bat, the first and probably the most accessible card to get if you are a student is a **credit card for students**. This is a bank-issued credit card. To apply, they will typically ask for your age, your class program, and you must be in an accredited university. If you are twenty years old or younger, then you need to have your mom, dad, or tutor be the primary applicant with you as the co-applicant. If you are twenty-one years or older, you won't need a co-applicant. This card is perfect for you if you are eighteen years old and are about to go to college. It's a straightforward way to start building your credit.

I'd advise checking with different banks for their rates and fees and if there are account-specific guidelines to follow. For example, a product readily available for Puerto Rico students is an Icon Visa card by Banco Popular de Puerto Rico. Although they automatically have a spending limit between $500 to $1,500, there's a catch. Every time your balance is under $200, the bank charges a fee. Details like this make a card better for you or can be a pain to have over time. Do your due diligence with every card.

These types of cards are great for starting credit. A very good friend of mine, Carlos Ayala, did not miss this opportunity to do exactly that. After his first day of college, he headed straight for the bank and was instantly approved. It wasn't much at first, but it was enough to buy the essentials. After some time, the bank automatically increased his limit. He told me, "It was great! They kept increasing my line of credit so often that when I threw my first college party, I charged most of it to that card. I still have that card to this day."

Student credit cards are an example of when you need a cosigner. A cosigner is usually someone who helps another person get access to credit rather than a primary borrower. This usually happens when you do not have any credit history and you're starting in the game. Whenever you go to a retail store that offers a credit card for its customers and apply for it without any credit history, you'll need a cosigner.

This happened to me, twice, while trying to get my first card. I went to Costco and Best Buy without any knowledge of what I was doing, applied, and got denied. Why is a cosigner necessary? Because they agree to accept liability for debts on the account if the primary borrower doesn't pay. Look at this as if it were a plan B if you do not pay. But there is a risk, like always. The borrower and cosigner have equal legal responsibility for repaying. If you do not, then both your credit scores are affected. The account activity shows up on both people's credit reports from the time the account is opened.

A **joint credit card account** is very similar to having a cosigner with a slight difference. While a cosigner acts as a backup when the primary borrower doesn't pay, a joint credit card account makes the two persons signing equally liable for the account. While most banks have moved away from these accounts, just know that this product is available to you.

A **secured credit card** will help you build credit at any point in your life. It is used for starting credit; for those who have a low credit score and banks don't want to loan money; and for those trying to rebuild credit after a setback. It is a great card, and it can be an invaluable tool. However, it is not your usual credit card where the bank issues you the card with a set credit limit for you to use.

Ulises Perez, my friend, professor at Sistema Universitario Ana G. Méndez, and business owner of LGMedia Group, NOI, and Los Gastrosóficos, has seen the value of secured credit cards. Because of the recent pandemic, Ulises missed some payments, lowering his credit and getting denied for new credit cards. He is using the secured credit card to rebuild his credit. "This card is literally saving my life. Since you told me this existed, it has helped me increase my credit score by sixty points in the last six months."

A secured credit card requires the applicant to provide a cash security deposit, usually your credit limit. The issuer then holds that deposit as collateral if you do not pay your bill. Then you can take the card and use it as you want it, as long as you pay. This type of card is more accessible to people with bad or no credit because it requires you to put money upfront to use it. The deposit protects the issuer from losing money.

In other words, you would go to the bank and ask them for a secured credit card, they usually ask for an amount higher than $250, you present the deposit, and *voilà!* You have your first credit card with a $250 line (credit limit). Make sure that your card issuer reports your activity to credit bureaus. As long as you pay on time and do not carry a balance, you can begin to strengthen your credit. You are now on your way to building an excellent credit history that will open the doors for better deals and perks and allow you to achieve financial freedom.

When looking around for secured credit cards, do not choose just any card. Choose a card that you can upgrade later during its lifetime. With some cards, you either have to keep open and lose the deposit, or, if you want the deposit back, you have to close the card, which will hurt the progress you made. So, when shopping for a card, look for one with a bank that will let you upgrade to a non-secured one.

The next path is becoming an **authorized user** on someone's credit card account. You might think that sounds like a joint account, but it isn't. In this case, only one person is responsible for all the debt accumulated on that account: the account owner. But being an authorized user lets you use someone else's credit card in your name. Once a person makes you an authorized user on their account, you will receive a credit card with your name on it. You will have access to that person's credit history, credit score, and debt.

The thing is, unlike the joint account, you are not legally responsible for paying any of the credit or debt the card builds up. This doesn't mean you can go out and be irresponsible with it, because that person's credit is now your credit. And if that person decides not to pay the debt, it will affect your credit too. The same thing happens if that person is responsible and pays; you will see your credit increase. The trick with this system is, and this will sound funny, to not use the card.

Most importantly, find someone you can trust, who is responsible with their credit, and has a healthy habit of credit management who will be willing to put you on their credit card line. Don't worry, adding you to the account will not affect the primary account holder's credit score, no matter your score, or lack of. Be smart about becoming an authorized user and choosing which person to help you out.

You may still read things like, "An account with a healthy score (740-plus) will help you get a step closer to better credit products and rates that you might not have otherwise qualified for." Mmm, not quite. Being an authorized user does nothing to your personal credit score. In the two newest versions of the FICO algorithm, authorized user accounts do not impact your FICO score. Why? Because they are not yours. You might see a rise in your vantage score when the authorized user card gets reported to the bureau, but that is it. It offers little to no help in the new scoring models.

Additionally, every major set of mortgage underwriting guidelines are required to disallow authorized user accounts from consideration. In other words, you can still do that, but it won't have any lasting effect in the near future. With the exception of being an authorized user, your chances of getting a card with a cashback perk or accumulating points for traveling are slim. Being an authorized user, you will receive the card that the principal account owner is holding, be it a Gold Amex or a Chase Freedom.

With that said, there is something you can do to have a higher chance of getting a better credit card product. First, start building your actual credit. Secondly, get a job. I'm not kidding. It helped me, and I'm sure it will help you. The following options are for those who have just started generating income and are looking for their first credit card.

As previously mentioned, **get a job.** It doesn't matter where it is or what you have to do, like managing an apartment or delivering food. The important thing here is to have a contract of employment. Once you have that down, make sure you've been at it for more than six months or get to the six-month mark. Most banks like to see that you have a contract of employment and that you have experience. You do not want to be seen as desperate for money and asking for a credit card the nex day after you signed your contract. It might tip off the bank.

Have you noticed that I've sent you to the bank in all of these cases and not to an online application? There is a reason for this. Most banks and credit entities will deny your application online due to the lack of credit history. On the other hand, visiting a bank lets you talk with a representative, tell them your situation, and negotiate a credit card for yourself. If you can't go to the bank, call customer service and wait until you talk with a bank representative before making any decision.

By negotiating, I mean determining the best card with the most perks they can offer. This approach will give you a chance to review the bank's credit cards before heading over and applying for a card. You should ask your bank representative which cards do not have an annual fee and have the lowest interest and annual percentage rate (APR). Since this is your first card, you do not want to pay a $95 annual fee. It isn't worth it.

To tell you the truth, I wish I had known that before going to the bank and making a fool of myself. Remember, I wanted to buy a house but couldn't because I didn't have any credit history. After getting denied, I headed home and started researching how to build credit. I did not investigate the banks and what products they had available to people without credit. Instead of going back to the same bank, I was naive, and I chose another bank to try my luck. Guess what happened? I got denied for the first time. Bam! I got a credit inquiry in my credit score before having any credit.

I thought to myself, *How can this be so difficult?* It is, but it isn't. That is what I am here for—to tell you how to do it right. Getting your first credit card is challenging if no one has taught you a bit about credit, the best time to start building credit, and how. Once you learn this, it then becomes effortless with the right information at hand, a good plan, and smart decisions.

I had no guidance whatsoever. My parents did not know how to teach me to start credit, even though they always pushed me to start it. And my friends were scared of even touching a credit card because of what society had been taught them. I became frustrated with the process of applying and getting denied over, and over, and over again. I applied to five different banks. What I did not know at the time was those five hard inquiries would show up in my credit history and stay there for two years. How did I notice? Well, after finally getting acceptance for my first credit card, I opened an account at Credit Karma, and there they were. Yes, they stayed there and held my credit score down for a while before falling off my credit history.

The next best thing for getting a credit card, and better than getting a job, is **starting your own business.** I know, I know, you might be thinking, this sounds crazy. But hang on a minute and check this out. Maybe you are not a regular employee, and instead you are an independent contractor, or you manage Airbnb, or sell plants on Instagram, or provide your services over Fiverr. Well, guess what? You already have a business, as far as the credit card companies are concerned. Now, you might be thinking, how is this possible? I just do this as a hobby or to earn extra money on the side. And all that is true.

You see, you are now considered self-employed, or a **sole proprietor.** In other words, the business and you are the same entity. There is no legal distinction between the company and you. The money you earn goes directly to your pocket, not to a corporate account in a bank. This is very well known, and you can take full advantage of it.

This is how I did it, though I did not intentionally start a business to get a credit card. My business has been running since 2015, operating in diverse projects from water treatment to business consulting. What happened to me was kind of weird and funny at the same time. In this scenario, when you go to the bank, they will ask you for employment proof.

In my case, instead of asking my boss for an employment letter or presenting them with my contract, I just needed to give them a letter that said how much time I've been in the company, what my salary was, when I started earning that, and a phone number to call and verify. The funny part is, since it's my business, I'm the owner, so I wrote my letter of employment. Sure, I did not sign it. Legally, I can't. But my mom did. They accepted the letter and asked me for a copy of my last two canceled checks.

To further prove my employment, they called the number on the letter. My mom answered the phone, answered the questions, and that was it. I was called the day after to go to the bank to sign the papers. Luckily, they did not ask to talk with my business partner. Between you and me, it's my dog. (Love you, Hotchi!)

This got me thinking, *If what I paid myself is the same amount in the letter, then it must be true.* I did not go back the next day with the canceled checks. Instead, I paid myself $1,000 more. And just to try it out, I went back to the bank, asked for the same bank representative who has been helping for the past months since the time I tried buying a house, and handed him the letter with the two recent canceled checks with $1,000 more. And it cleared out. Yes, amazing. This is happening.

Then, a weird thing happened to me. The bank representative told me that the total I was making was $3,500 a month, but he couldn't give me that. To make sure I did not spend all of my income on the credit card, the bank took 15 percent of my income in the credit limit calculation, leaving me with a credit limit of $3,000. Not bad for a first card and compared to the $500 I'd most probably get by any other method. So, I agreed.

They proceeded to tell me that the bank had three different credit cards that they could offer me. One that earned points for their catalog and one that earned points for traveling and has an annual fee. The third was a basic one. Which do you guess I chose? Wrong. I chose two! I did not know what I was doing. I just wanted more cards. In the long run, this was a reasonable mistake.

If you go back to the average age of the account category, what does it say? Total months of opened accounts divided by number of accounts. And this is for all your opened accounts. You can see this information in your credit card's platform. They all offer a tool that tells you your spending habits for the month. This also helps you determine what your next card should be.

In my case, I spend most of my money on food and gas. I travel a lot around the whole island of Puerto Rico and enjoy the food every place has to offer, from *bistec encebolla'o* in Aguadilla to *carne frita*, *longaniza*, and *tostones* in Orocovis. So, ideally, my next card should be one that gives me the most points for dining out and gas stations. I did some research and found out that Discover offered what I was looking for.

By this point, I had been reading and studying about credit and credit cards for a while. Before applying for the Discover card, I did a little exercise with my credit history. It said that I had nine months of average credit age. Using the division from above, if I was accepted for the card now, my average age of credit would drop to four and a half (or four) months. But I had two cards, not one. This is how my mistake worked out. Having two cards and an average age of nine months meant that I had nine months of credit on each of my cards.

The math is as follows: the age of credit card one plus the age of credit card two divided by total accounts, or 9 + 9 / 2 = 9 months average credit. Using that same division, if I opened a new credit card today, then it would be 9 + 9 + 0 / 3 = 6. By having a second card and then adding a third, my score would stay at six months and wouldn't drop to four months like I had originally thought. This is the importance of having a couple of credit cards in your history. It will not only hold your average age of credit up, but it will provide you stability when taking a hit on your credit score.

The last product I'd advise getting is a **store credit card**, like Best Buy, Sephora, or Costco. You probably will need a cosigner for this. Either way, the perks the cards offer are often store-specific and do not offer anything special. You can't even use some cards outside the store. This type of card is useful once you have established credit and need to buy expensive items. They usually offer 0 percent interest for the first twelve to fifteen months. Almost every big retailer has its own credit card. Some examples are Sally Beauty, Shell Gas, Amazon, West Elm, and Lowes, to name a few.

The past options are geared toward credit cards. If you cannot or do not want a credit card to start your credit history, that is okay. Here is the next best thing for you: a **credit builder loan.** This loan aims to put the money you borrowed into an account and make your principal and interest payments, then the bank will report your payments to the bureaus. This type of loan is geared toward those who do not have credit and are looking to build it or for those in the rebuilding phase of their credit. It works great in both circumstances.

Typically, the lender on an account holds the amount of money you want to borrow until the loan is repaid. In the meantime, you contribute to the loan through payments every month that the lender is then reporting to the credit bureaus. It's like a forced savings program. Once the loan is repaid, the lender then releases the money in your account with full access. Keep in mind that this type of loan, like any other, will incur interest. Do your diligence and check the rates.

CreditStrong.com is a great platform to start with. When you sign up, you open a savings account with them. Then, you start paying (or more like contributing) a monthly deposit to your account. They then report your payments to your account as paying off the debt. It's that simple. Loan terms are between one to two years and some have a minimum monthly payment. The higher your monthly payment, the higher a credit limit or loan amount you can ask for in the future.

Another option in this area is Self.inc. They work the same way. You open an account with them and start depositing funds every month that the company will report as payments. This way, you start saving some money while building credit. At the end of the loan term, you can either withdraw the funds or leave them there as a savings account. Either way, you have now built credit and your savings.

Other companies offer this same service, but with a caveat. They do two things differently. They give you the funds first, and then you pay them back. Sounds great, right? It actually is. You don't have to put any money up front to start with them. And that is exactly the problem.

Instead of choosing a sizable amount of money to pay monthly, say $100 or $200, you are stuck with their terms.

Sure, they will entice you with low monthly payments of $15, which is great if you are strapped for money. But here is the problem of low monthly payments like that: Let's say you want to take out a $20,000 loan for your business. When banks start the underwriting process, where they assess their financial risk, they will look at your credit report. I'm sure it will be excellent. But when they focus on your loan, they will be worried. They will be able to loan you the $20,000 for five years. That comes to a monthly payment of $333 for sixty months. But they will not be sure if you can pay them back. Why? Because your report shows that you have only paid $15 a month for a loan. That is a long way from $333. And thus, they probably will not approve the loan.

On the other hand, $150 is closer to $300. Banks will have an easier time approving you for that same loan. At the same time, if you have a history of paying $800 a month for a loan, your chances of getting approved for a higher loan amount are better.

As mentioned before, a loan is very similar to a secured credit card, a "buy yourself or your family member something" loan. It is a variation of the credit builder loan, but instead the bank is lending you the money and holding it in an account. At the same time, you pay it in full, you already have the money in an account, and you use it as collateral to buy something while still making the payments.

These are very direct and straightforward options for building and rebuilding your credit. Check the interest rates on them and make sure they are the lowest. Determine a loan term that is less than twenty-four months, which is usually twelve months. Make the payments, on time, every time. This is for your benefit only. Do not screw it up. While starting your credit, a missed payment will linger in your credit history for seven years and hold your credit score down.

Throughout this chapter, you have seen that credit cards, loans, and authorized users have one thing in common: paying on time, every time. Some options don't require you to pay because you are not the primary owner of the account, but getting into the habit will help you build your credit and achieve financial freedom. For the rest of the options, paying on time is key to building a strong credit history and a high credit score. It is a habit that you should practice for both credit cards and loans. Tie that habit with not carrying a balance. Only using your card when you have the cash will take you many more steps closer to your desired financial freedom.

"I don't use a debit card. The safest thing is a credit card because you're using the bank's money. If someone accesses your information, they are stealing the bank's money, not yours."
—FRANK ABAGNALE [35]

One recent company has opened the doors for those not yet able to apply for a credit card or loan: Experian. You have heard of them in this book, maybe while reading credit-related articles, and probably recently on YouTube ads and TV. They offer an Experian Boost. When you sign

---

35   Michael Mulcahy II, "Fraught with Fraud: Tips for Increasing Your Digital Security," Kings Path Partners, April 3, 2020.

up for free with them, choose this option. It is a way to have your cell phone and utility bills count toward your credit score. Permit them to connect with your bank account, and they automatically identify the cell phone and utility bill payments. On top of this, they will only report your on-time payments, meaning that your late payments will not show up in your credit report, which is very different from what we have talked about.

One last piece of advice: If you are rejected for any of the products, the bank or issuer will tell you why. And that is great. The same reason that checking your credit score often to see where you stand and know what you have to work on, the bank's feedback is excellent to understand why you were rejected and what you need to do to get accepted.

Some cards, which I did not include here, guarantee approval without first checking your credit score. While that might sound great, there is always a catch in the form of high-interest rates or high fees, and probably both. The other card is a prepaid one. Avoid them at all costs. They do nothing for your credit score.

Do not give up. Ask the bank if you can qualify for a card or a loan in other ways, preferably in the bank, but if not then over the phone. Some consider payment history from rental and utility records, like Experian, for their products. You will not know until you ask.

As a recap, this is how I started building credit and how I helped my brother build his. In my case, I had a job for more than six months. With a written letter of employment (some banks may ask for your employment contract) and the check receipts of my last two payments, I asked the bank teller to check what credit cards he could offer me. I pre-qualified for three, so I took two. I put $2,000 on the card I would be using the most, and the rest on the card I knew I'd be using the least. This was a great decision in the long run because of two reasons: 1) I started with two cards, which helped my credit build faster; and 2) I had two cards with only one hard inquiry. You can see the benefit in that. Six months later I was taking out my third card with no problem.

Take my approach if you are employed. In my brother's case while building a startup, he still does not have the cash flow to pay himself every month. So first, I added him as an authorized user on one of my mom's credit cards (sorry Dad, Mom had a higher credit score thank you). Secondly, and around the same time, he took out a secured credit card for $500. Neither of these actions negatively impact my brother or my mom. There was no hard inquiry for the authorized user in mom's report nor in my brother's report for the authorized user. Remember, the authorized user card is to have something in your report. That credit history is not your own. That is why he opened a secured credit card: to show the banks he is good at paying back the borrowed money.

One credit product to add in your first two years of building credit is a personal loan no matter the amount as long as the loan has a minimum term of twenty-four months. This will hugely benefit your credit score. It will show that you can consistently pay a loan for two years. It will also help your total accounts segment to add a personal loan on top of your credit cards in your credit mix. You can find personal loans online, in banks, and in cooperatives of savings and credit. People often forget about them, when in fact they play a huge role in the community since they do not operate the same way as federal banks do. They are ruled by local governing statutes.

Henry M. Paulson, former CEO of Goldman Sachs and Secretary of the Treasury from 2006 to 2009, emphasizes the role cooperatives have in consumers and small businesses when he said, "Non-bank financial institutions provide credit that is essential to US businesses and consumers."[36]

A cooperative, or credit union, is a "**people-centered enterprise** owned, controlled and run by and for their members to realize their common economic, social, and cultural needs and aspirations."[37] In other words, a type of bank where everyone who has an account with them is a stakeholder in the business. That means that every year, they get dividends for trusting and investing their money with them. There are different cooperatives for your needs. You can find a small business-oriented cooperative, where they provide extended benefits for business owners, or land development cooperatives and even agricultural cooperatives, among others.

A big advantage cooperatives and credit unions have over big banks is that they are community based. Thus, they help the community prosper. You can find competitive rates for mortgages and car loans in your local cooperative. And even if every other bank denies your credit

---

36   "U.S. Department of the Treasury," Remarks by Secretary Henry M. Paulson, Jr. on Financial Rescue Package and Economic Update, December 14, 2020.

37   "What Is a Cooperative?" ICA, accessed December 30, 2020.

application, your local cooperative can help out. They are also a great tool to rebuild your credit. Do not rule them out.

A couple of things you can do right now to get started: Call or go online and check out any of the starting products we talked about. Once you know which one you like, go ahead and apply. I recommend going straight to the credit cards if you can show proof of employment. If you can't, you can start with a secured credit card and add a credit builder loan along the way. Any of those two options will get you started in building your credit.

To learn more and compare the different products available to you, visit me at LuccianoDiazSkoff.com and reach out on Instagram @LuccianoDiazSkoff.

CHAPTER 6.

All This Money?
Is It Mine?

———

"Money is only a tool. It will take you wherever you wish, but it will not replace you as the driver."

—AYN RAND

Now that you are on the path to achieving financial freedom through credit cards, you will possibly have quite a lot of them and a lot of credit at your disposal. The amount of credit you will be able to use is the sum of all your credit limits, including any amount already borrowed.

Your available credit, on the other hand, is all the difference between the credit limit and the account balance, or in other words, how much you have left to spend. Available credit and credit limit might be better interpreted as the relationship that exists between your current spending power and the total spending power. That spending power is determined by each card issuer the moment you apply for a card.

They do this through a very complex process called underwriting. Underwriting is the process through which an individual or institution takes on financial risk for a fee.[38] This is a set of very complex mathematical formulas, testing, and analysis.

The term "underwriting" originated from the practice of having each risk-taker write their name under the total amount of risk they were willing to accept for a specified premium. Although the mechanics have changed over time, underwriting continues today as a key function in the financial world. The details of the functions, equations, and procedures are private, since that's how banks make money.

This computational analysis helps the company decide who to approve, at what rate, and at what limit. This goes for credit cards, loans, insurance, and investments alike, including everything in between. If the underwriting is too high, the bank can refuse to issue a loan or extend coverage. Nonetheless, the higher the credit limit the underwriting assigns, the more the company trusts the borrower to repay the debt.

It works the other way around too. To keep things simple, banks have product tiers. In our case, they have credit card tiers. The cards you find per tier are ultimately arranged using two indicators: your credit history and your income. Banks have different cards for different credit scores, or the lack thereof, and different incomes. You can choose to apply to any of the cards a credit issuer can offer, but those two determining factors will be the ones to tell which product offers the less risk for the issuer.

---

38   Caroline Banton, "How Underwriters Assess the Risk of Insurers," *Investopedia*, September 10, 2020.

If you have no credit score but some income, you have your tier one cards. Your tier two and tier three cards are alongside incomes between $20,000 to $40,000 with your credit score determining the tier. And for your fourth tier, a high credit score or a high income, depending on both, will determine if a card in that tier will suit you well.

Don't get me wrong, you can apply for a good card with a great credit score and a medium income. An example of this is the Amex Gold card or the Chase Sapphire Preferred (CSP). The two are great cards with even better perks.

A great friend of mine was recently approved for the CSP and shared her story with me. Natalia Bellaflores had just moved back to the island during the pandemic and wanted to start a business with her family. The biggest hurdle was getting access to starting capital. Instead of going to the banks, she decided to get a credit card. She applied with a medium salary and got approved for a $7,500 credit line instantly. Why? She has an average credit history of six years, with the oldest account being ten years old. Mind you, she only has her student loan and one credit card in her report with no negative factors.

In her case, her credit score did the heavy lifting in the decision, not her income. This is the importance of keeping your oldest accounts open and giving your credit history time to grow. Soon, the bank will see that she is responsible, and they surely will bump up her credit limit 10 to 20 percent.

Natalia used her new credit card to buy the essentials for the business and have money to operate. Nowadays, Natalia and her parents are the proud owners of Mar y Trova in the beautiful coast of Salinas, Puerto Rico. You can find me there every other Sunday indulging in their famous vegan *alcapurrias* and *empanadillas.*

When making a decision, issuers like to see your complete credit report. They factor in the rest using your payment history, your average age of credit and length of credit history, and the number of credit accounts you have on your report. These include student loans, mortgages, auto loans, and accounts of the like as well as your inquiries.

This is all part of your credit report—or financial resume—that you can get a free copy every year from each of the bureaus at AnnualCreditReport.com. To stay up to date with the health of your credit, I recommend downloading one or two free apps with weekly and monthly updates on your progress. You can see how each of the categories we talked about influence the banks', cards', issuers', and credit unions' decision on extending you credit. It all ties together, and it can work for you or against you, depending on how well you know how to play the game.

A little hack that might help you get a higher credit limit on your cards is having high credit limits on each of your cards in your report. Although you may not need more than $500 on a credit card, that might affect your next card's limit. The underwriting process, the process where a credit issuer determines your credit limit, varies from company to company. Some issuers like to check each of your cards' limit in your report as a way of knowing what other people have risked lending you. So, having a card with a $5,000 limit, even though you do not use it often, might help you in the future.

Credit card issuers like to know how good of a borrower you are. That is the reason for your credit score. By comparing if other lenders saw something on your credit report that might have changed their mind or if others have extended credit to you, they might have an idea if you are good at borrowing money or not.

Another point that some lenders take into account is your debt-to-income (DTI) ratio, one of the reasons a credit card issuer might have turned down your credit card application. The DTI ratio is a comparison between an individual's monthly debt payment and their monthly gross income.[39] The ratio shows, in a percentage, how much of your monthly income goes to paying your monthly debt payments.

If you use your card without having the cash, not paying in full and on time and then carrying a balance you pay at least a minimum amount monthly, gets you a high DTI ratio. Again, if you follow the simple rules, this ratio will be 0 percent by the time you apply for another card.

Beware, banks do take into account this ratio when asking for a car loan or a mortgage. They do this to know how much money you have left after you have paid your debt and taxes. They take into account the money left, not your gross income, to calculate how much you can pay for a mortgage. It is important to know your money limits.

With your credit limit determined, there are two good things that can happen next. Usually, credit card issuers reevaluate a credit cardholder's credit limit every six to twelve months. They look at your credit utilization rate,

39 Chris B. Murphy, "How Lenders and Banks Use Your Debt-to-Income (DTI) Ratio," *Investopedia*, September 22, 2020.

or your on-time monthly payments, including paying your balance in full. Some issuers increase your credit limit upon reevaluation of your excellent credit history. Others simply tell you that you qualify for a credit limit increase.

There is no hard inquiry in your credit report when the credit issuer bumps up your credit limit automatically. However, when they tell you that you qualify for a credit limit increase, you should always ask if this means getting a hard inquiry on your credit report. If it doesn't, then happily get the credit limit increase. If it does, ponder the weight of having a hard inquiry for a credit limit increase or saving the hard inquiry for a card you want.

"A credit card is a convenient device that saves you the trouble of counting your change."

—EVAN ESAR[40]

One card that automatically increases your credit limit is American Express. Yes, they do, and more regularly than you imagine. American Express has two different cards: a charge card and a credit card. We have talked about both. This time, I'm talking about their charge card. A charge card is a card with no pre-set spending limit. However, this does not mean unlimited spending.

Your purchasing power varies with the use of your card. Amex takes into account your payment history, credit score, income, and other sources to determine that purchasing power. The charge card, unlike the credit card, has to be paid in full every month. Fortunately, you do not have to pay interest, since you pay your balance in full

---

40   "Evan Esar Quote," *AZQuotes*, accessed August 18, 2020.

every month. Although, they do have fees for late payments and charge interest in the "pay over time" feature. Why all the fuss about Amex anyway? Why does everyone want an Amex, besides its perks and flexible spending limit? Here is where it gets interesting. Because Amex does not have a pre-set spending limit on their charge cards, they do not report a credit limit, thus allowing you to rank up a considerable amount of charges without affecting your utilization rate. In other words, you never carry a balance because you have to pay in full and on time, which does not increase your utilization rate.

I must warn you about this advantage: It may work against you. Having a card that does not report a credit limit is great but having revolving credit near or at their limits might be harmful to your credit score. The intention of using another card with a credit limit is lowering your utilization rate and your payments. The charge card will do you no good in that situation. Getting accepted for a charge card with a credit limit of $10,000 will not lower your credit utilization rate. Since Amex does not report a credit limit to bureaus, your new $10,000 credit line will not affect your current utilization rate.

Be smart about your situation and how different cards, no matter how good they are, help you out. The best way to use a charge card is to have all your other cards at zero or minimum spending and use the charge card for everyday things, thus keeping your utilization rate at 0 percent even though using "90 percent" of your Amex spending limit. Remember, this is only true with charge cards.

The way that Amex increases your purchasing power varies from person to person. Expect to have a very low credit limit if it is your first Amex card. In the first month, put some charges on the card and pay in full and on time. Then every month, do the same, increasing the amount you charge on the card, consecutively. In no time they will see that every month you were close to their "credit limit," and with your on-time payments and no balance, they will be comfortable in increasing your purchasing power every so often, even maybe every month.

You can see why American Express has a great reputation amongst credit cardholders. They have some of the best credit card perks, features, and status, and they have the second-best customer satisfaction in the US. Add that to the ever-increasing, not pre-set credit limit, you can guess why everybody wants an American Express. In my experience, their customer service is impeccable and is second to none.

A quick note on increasing credit limits: If you are offered a credit limit increase in a card that you already have an ongoing balance, accruing interest rates and fees, and you have been trying to pay it down without success, most likely a credit limit increase will do you more harm than good. A higher credit limit lowers your overall credit utilization rate, this is still true in this case. What is different is the amount of debt the person has on that one card.

If you have been trying to lower your debt for months, what do you think will happen when the bank increases your credit line to $5,000? You will most probably increase your debt, therefore increasing your minimum monthly payments and your fees. You will be trapped in your own cycle of spending. In this case, wait until you have paid most, if not all, of your credit card debt to accept your credit limit increase. You are the master of your cards; you have the control. Do not let them control you.

"Capital as such is not evil; it is its wrong use that is evil. Capital in some form or other will always be needed." [41]

—MOHANDAS KARAMCHAND GANDHI

Being a responsible spender, having a low utilization rate, paying in full and on time, and not carrying a balance will be fruitful in increasing your credit score. Your credit limit does not matter that much when you have a couple of cards in your wallet, nor when you are starting out. The lesson here is how much purchasing power you have, and that comes with credit limits and credit mix.

To calculate your current utilization rate, learn how to lower it, and grasp how a credit limit increase will affect you, visit me at LuccianoDiazSkoff.com and reach out on Instagram @LuccianoDiazSkoff.

---

41   "Mahatma Gandhi," Oxford Reference, accessed September 19, 2020.

CHAPTER 7.

Moving Up

—

"The next step in sculpture is motion."

—ALEXANDER CALDER

Let's talk about your second card and everything that comes with it. You just got your first card, and it feels great! It comes as no surprise that it feels different than handling cash and doesn't have the same effect and texture. Beware of that feeling though, as most people go out spending beyond their means and end in ruin.

As you know, your hard-earned money, your cold hard cash, is the physical equivalent of your time. In other words, the time you invested in an action has a return of investment not in time, but in money. When you take it out of your wallet, count it, and pay with it, you are counting the time you put in to earn it. But paying with plastic makes it easier to lose that perspective. It makes it less painful, because you are not thinking about what that card represents, other than carrying fewer things in your wallet.

That is when most people stumble into debt. They stop respecting the relationship the credit card has with cash and with your credit. They swipe it endlessly with the illusion of having money in the account or working for it later. This is not the way to go about using your credit card.

A credit card is a tool that will bring you financial freedom if you are smart. Taking a credit card for granted and swiping it endlessly will bury you in debt without your awareness. Like Robert Kiyosaki said, "More important than the how we achieve financial freedom, is the why. Find your reasons why you want to be free and wealthy."[42]

Always keep in mind the three rules: Use your credit card only if you have the cash, never carry a balance, and always pay in full and on time. Follow these rules and you won't have to worry about your credit score as it will only keep increasing.

By now you must have gotten a letter in the mail with your card and how to activate it. Inside are the terms and conditions of using your card. The five most important things are the credit limit, the card's annual fee, if any, the APR offered, foreign transaction fees, and late fees. Other than the card's credit limit, the rest are fees which you should know and understand.

The credit limit, as previously mentioned, is the limit assigned to that card after the application process while the bank is reviewing your request. Do not worry about the limit with your first card, because you can ask for a credit limit increase later. Some cards actually increase it periodically. Those cards usually have an annual fee. Why would a card have an annual fee? Because of perks.

_____
42   "Robert Kiyosaki Quote," AZQuotes, accessed October 19, 2020.

It's all about the perks, features, welcome bonuses, and rewards. Annual fees range from $95 to $650, with some very exclusive cards with an annual fee of $5,000 and an initiation fee of $10,000. That's a lot of dough for a card. What it brings for that amount of money, though, is sometimes worth it.

Take for example Chinese billionaire Liu Yiqian. He used his American Express card to buy a painting for $170 million, collecting 422 million Amex points, converting them to twenty-eight million frequent flyer miles, which translates to $180,000 worth of vouchers.[43] You can guess he will never have to pay for another airplane ticket again.

The card with a $5,000 annual fee and the one used for that transaction is the American Express Centurion card, or "Black Card." This card is by invitation only. They recently opened a portal where you can submit your request to be evaluated for it. Requirements for approval are not public, but based on other users' reports, you need to charge between $250,000 and $500,000 a year with your current American Express card. This charge depends on whether you are the only one using the card, it is a joint card, or it's a business card.

If you are approved for the Black Card, the benefits are great. You can lock in hotel elite status at Marriott, Hilton, Intercontinental Hotels Group, and Relais & Châteaux. This gets you late check out times, free room upgrades, spa credits, and free breakfast. You will have elite status at airlines. That includes bonus miles, in-air perks, and complimentary upgrades. While waiting for the flight,

---

43   Associated Press, "Billionaire Earns First-Class Travel for Life by Putting Modigliani Nude on Amex," Guardian News and Media, November 24, 2015.6

you can use the card to access more than 1,200 airport lounges around the world. These provide personal space, individual showers, good food and drinks, working stations, and even a room to nap if a flight is delayed. Other perks include Equinox gym membership, $1,000 per year credit in Saks Fifth Avenue, TSA Pre-Check, International arrival service, and no spending limit.

The most amazing perk of all, making it stand out from all other cards, is the twenty-four seven concierge service. Yes. You have a dedicated line to call, and an Amex concierge will pick up and work with you and your needs.[44]

Another card worth mentioning is the J.P. Morgan Reserved card. This card is reserved only for those who have at least $10 million in assets with J.P. Morgan Private Bank. The perks? You can expect the best of the best of credit card perks from the bank. It is a status symbol with a $595 annual fee.[45] Now, let's go back to the real world.

The annual fee, like any other fee, will still lower your credit score if not paid. Likewise, APR (annual percentage rate) is the interest rate you'll pay on the balance you carry from month to month. We know how to avoid these. If you carry over a balance, the APR will apply to you. Know that, when carrying a balance, a **minimum payment** is required. This is the lowest amount you can pay on your credit card to avoid penalties, not fees. You still need to make a payment, and the minimum the

44   Dia Adams, "American Express Centurion Black Card 2020 Review," *Forbes Magazine,* July 21, 2020.

45   Brett Holzhauer, Brett Holzhauer, and Brett Holzhauer, "J.P. Morgan Reserve Card (Formerly Chase Palladium): Everything You Need to Know," ValuePenguin, accessed December 30, 2020.

bank is requesting is that set amount. If you don't, they will report it to the credit bureaus, and you will have a derogatory mark in your credit history.

Banks typically give you around 30 days to pay the balance from the last month. If you cannot pay the balance, or the minimum, late fees and interest start applying.[46] This is the reason it is important to pay your balance in full and on time.

Falling back on payments will result in carrying a balance for months, increasing the minimum payments, and adding late fees and interest. If you do not pay within those thirty days, it is up to the bank's discretion to mark that month as no payment and try collecting the payment themselves. Some banks give additional grace periods of sixty and ninety days before reporting your account to bureaus as delinquent. When one hundred twenty day have passed and no payment has been made to that account whatsoever, banks report your account as a charge-off (as bad debt for tax purposes). In that case, collection agencies come after you.

On top of all of that, an increased utilization rate and more interest accrue. Those are known as late fees. These are charged when you pay one day late or do not pay at least the minimum amount due. As with the rules of the credit game, the fees in a credit card are all intertwined.

The last fees are foreign transaction fees which, of course, mean the fees charged when making purchases outside the US. All of these are the penalties for misusing your credit card, which not only translates into paying

---

46 Bev O'Shea, "How Does a Late Payment Affect Your Credit?" NerdWallet, December 16, 2020.

more to cover the fees, but your credit score and history are affected too. Do not be surprised after seeing all of these fees even when you haven't yet used your card.

The knowledge you have acquired from reading this book will have you using your credit card, increasing your credit score, and reaching the financial freedom you want for yourself.

"Money is a terrible master but an excellent servant."[47]

—P.T. BARNUM

You may have heard or read that when starting to build your credit and applying to your first credit card, you should wait two years to apply for another card and no less than one year for a credit limit increase. It happened to me when I got my first card.

The teller advised me to go back to the bank after one year if I was still interested in another card. He further advised that having too many cards is not good for my credit. I was surprised to hear this from someone who should be educating people.

I sat down again to read even more about credit and credit cards, and what I found was outstanding. What we have been hearing all our life, how "having too many cards is bad," "wait two years to apply," and more, is totally wrong! You've now read how many credit accounts or products you need to have a good ranking in the category—which is eleven. The time between cards is also false. There is actually no set time limit to apply for your second card,

---

47   "Forbes Quotes," Forbes (Forbes Magazine), accessed September 19, 2020.

or third, or how many cards you want for that matter. But you do have to be smart about when to apply.

Usually, banks estimate two years before you will have a good credit score and credit history. You can do that as early as your first month. By the time the card lands on your doorstep, you have opened your credit history. And when a month passes and you've made your first payment, your score will show that the first month of your credit history you did not miss a payment and your utilization rate is 0 percent.

Theoretically, you can apply for another card after that first month, although it is not recommended due to the lack of experience in your credit history. Banks also take their time reporting to the credit bureaus. When is it a good time then? It will vary for each one of you.

I would recommend that once you have paid on time for six months and your credit utilization rate is 0 percent then you increase your chances of being approved. It is the same situation involving a credit limit increase. As long as you have a substantial credit history, go for it. Please remember that a credit limit increase requires a hard pull on your credit score most of the time, and approval is not automatic. So before making a decision, ponder on the benefits of having more credit available to you on a single credit card or more credit in the form of an extra credit card with perks. It is up to you.

Typically, banks offer you a higher credit limit around a year after you opened your card. This happens because they see that you actively use and take advantage of your card. Another way banks offer a credit limit increase is by asking you if your income has changed. If it has and you can prove it, they will gladly approve your credit limit increase. Usually, when banks offer you a credit limit increase, they did not do a hard pull in your credit. When you ask for a limit increase, they pull your credit. Make sure your bank tells you if they do or do not pull your credit. This will help your decision making too.

"The key to using credit cards effectively is to pay off your credit card in full every month."[48]

—RAMIT SETHI

What might be a good second credit card? The one that fits your needs. Your first credit card helped lay the foundation where your credit builds. Most likely, it will be your longest account open on your credit history. Even though it does not have any perks, you will never cancel the card. You will simply store it away in a drawer and use it once or twice a year to avoid getting it closed.

With your second credit card, on the other hand, you can venture out of the basic category. Let us call this your first tier. First-tier cards are the cards that help you build credit, usually don't offer perks, and have no annual fee.

Your second-tier credit cards are the ones that will allow you to start gaining access to some of the perks and features of better cards. These cards do not have an annual fee and earn you points. Examples of these are the Chase Freedom, Discover it, and the Amex Everyday card, among others.

The next tier of cards, tier three, is where things start to get interesting. You will start seeing more rewards and

---

48   Ramit Sethi, *I Will Teach You to Be Rich: No Guilt, No Excuses, No BS - Just a 6-Week Programme That Works* (New York: Workman, 2020). 58

higher sign-up bonuses. Although some of these cards have an annual fee, they really allow you to earn numerous points for airlines, hotels, and more.

Some examples of these cards are the Chase Sapphire Preferred and the American Express Gold. Some airlines offer cards as well, which come with a free checked bag, priority boarding, and coupons to access airport lounges. Hotel cards are also included in this tier. They come with sign up bonuses and have upgraded user status in their hotels; in other words, the ability for early check-in, late check-out, discounts, and much more.

Tier four cards are as prestigious as it can get for most people. Cards like American Express Platinum and Chase Sapphire Reserve offer their users exceptional perks on airline miles and premium airport lounge access. On top of that, you get huge cash back, travel and ride credits, and often better member status in hotels. But while sign up bonuses are not that significantly higher, the annual fees sure are.

Most of these cards strike your eye due to their design and weight, most being made from metal instead of plastic. Another card made from metal is the American Express Centurion card, or the "Black Card." This card is in a tier of its own with two or three others. They are the most exclusive, invitation-only cards. To get invited to apply you must have a ridiculously high income and ridiculous expenses. These are your tier five cards and the epitome of credit card status. But, before we can get to the holy grail, we must choose your second card.

For your second card, there are many categories to choose from. The first category is a no annual fee card. Cards in this category are the best cards all around since you do not have to worry about paying the card every year and missing a payment. These cards often have some cash-back perks in quarterly categories or specific categories throughout the year. Some offer points you can use to buy flights or products through the bank's partners. Discover, for example, has a card that matches the cash back you have earned at the end of the year. This is an example of a good cash-back card with no annual fee.

Our second category of cards we can choose from is cash-back cards. Almost every bank offers one of these. They are one of the most widely used cards along with point cards. Cash-back cards are very popular since they are easy to use, the rewards are straightforward, and everybody loves them. The con of cash-back cards, which is the pro of point cards, is that they do not offer travel perks. So if you do not travel a whole lot, getting cash back will suit you well. If you do travel, a points card that you can combine with other and better cards from the same bank will get you the best bang for your points in flights and hotels.

With some cards, you do not have to wait for the year to pass to get that cash-back match bonus. They offer a sign-up bonus you can later redeem for miles, which is normally three months after you get your card. This brings us to the cards that will give you the most out of flying and airport lounge access. These cards are products mostly from airlines looking for that frequent flyer as a customer, which is not bad if you are going to really use the miles.

Other credit products aimed at frequent flyers are hotel cards. Whereas airline cards give you miles, hotel cards provide you the comfort of being a member of the hotel chain and partners around the globe. You can usually get this status and use the points with other cards in exchange for a stay.

A well-known card combo is the Chase trifecta, or the Amex trifecta. This is when you have three key cards from the same bank and use them in a way that supplements each other in maximizing your points.

How does this work? In Chase's case, you have the new Chase Freedom Flex (FF), the Freedom Unlimited (FU), and the Chase Sapphire Reserve (CSR). The FF gives you 5 percent on rotating quarterly categories, 3 percent in dining and drugstores, and 1 percent in everything else. The FU does not have quarterly categories but does have a 1.5 percent on every purchase. What you would do is use the FF in the categories each quarter and while dining and in drugstores (FU also gives the same 3 percent in dining and drugstores). But instead of using the FF for every other purchase, you use the FU that has 1.5 percent in that category. That's 0.5 percent more! The CSR, on the other hand, gives you ten-times the points on Lyft rides. After you have gathered all your points you can send them all to the CSR portal and redeem them for 50 percent more value. With that, you buy your flights, hotels, and more.

The Amex Trifecta works the same way. You have three cards, each with its own special category, and you maximize each to get the most out of your card. Once you get to the desired goal, you can transfer all the points that will give you more value for points and the most perks. For Amex, you would use the Blue Business Plus, Amex

Gold, and Platinum cards. It is fair to mention that these cards are not the exact ones to have. You can change them to your benefit and lifestyle. You can even have four cards in the "Trifecta plus one card" combo. The idea here is to have that set of cards that, when combined, give you the most value for your points. You choose which works best for you.

Balance transfer, 0 percent APR, and low-interest cards are perfect if you have a debt or are planning to have one. Balance transfer cards are a great tool to pay that debt that has been bugging you for quite a while. This is not magic, nor a trick; this is a way of getting out of paying interest, lowering your credit card utilization rate, and paying your debt.

When you get a balance transfer card, you ask the issuer of the card to own your debt. In other words, you transfer one outstanding balance from one card to the other. The bank consolidates your debt with the bank owning the balance.

Most of the time, these cards come with an introductory 0 percent APR for twelve or fifteen months. This is great for you! You have fifteen months of not having to worry about interest rates while you pay your debt. Zero percent APR cards are great if you are about to buy something that you know will take you some time to pay off.

In this case, buying it with this card relieves you of the worry of paying interest for the amount of time the card sets. It is a great way of not paying extra for what you just bought. However, when the 0 percent APR introductory period ends, your normal interest will kick in. We do not want that, so be sure to pay your card in full before that happens.

The same is true with low-interest cards. If you know you will have a debt that will take some time to pay off, a low-interest card with 0 percent APR for some time will help pay that debt. Then, use the card with the lowest APR to make the purchase.

The last two credit card categories are no foreign transaction fees and business credit cards. No foreign transaction fees will help you out of not having to pay the usual 3 percent when using your card outside the country of origin.

Some credit cards from international banks like Banco Santander, who is based in Spain with branches throughout the world, do not charge you a fee for using the card in places they have a presence. For example, even though I have a Banco Santander card from Puerto Rico, I do not have to pay any fees when using it in Argentina or Germany.

Lastly, and how the name suggests, business cards are aimed at businesses. Although these cards are for the business, they carry the business owner's name, since the credit score the bank uses for the business credit card is the owner's.

It is a very exciting feeling to have so many options to choose from to keep building your credit and achieving your financial freedom. When you choose your next card and apply for it, make sure to have no missed payments and 0 percent utilization rate. This, in combination with the other aspects of your credit score, will draw higher chances of getting approved.

Do not forget to use the pre-qualified tool that some credit card issuers and webpages offer to know if you qualify. This tool will help you avoid an unnecessary hard inquiry. Most importantly, always follow the three rules: Use your card if you have the cash, always pay in full and on time, and do not carry a balance. This is a bulletproof way of getting the credit score you want.

Now, get ready to apply for your second card. A card that I completely love is the Discover it Chrome card. This card gives me 2 percent cash back in gas and restaurants, plus the match at the end of the year. I chose this card specifically because it ties perfectly to my lifestyle. Most of the time I am on the road traveling around Puerto Rico in my truck. As you know, trucks have an appetite for gas.

Furthermore, my work demands me to meet with business owners, mostly restaurants and bars, where I frequently find myself grabbing a bite or a beer with the business owners. These two activities are the most recurring and common ones to use my card. So I chose a card that ties into all of that. You can see how this card benefits me.

You should do the same thing too. Sit down and evaluate what things you spend more on. At the time I took out this card I had six months of credit history and a credit score of seven hundred thirty-eight (FICO Score 8 based on TransUnion data). Make a list of the three or four things you spend the most money on and start picking cards for each category. When you see a card that repeats itself every time, you got your next card.

If you don't, choose the category of things you spend the most money on and the cards that give you the best benefits in that category. Once you have the list of cards, go one by one evaluating the other benefits. Find one that has the most benefits for you. You will know.

A second card represents an opportunity to expand your credit history and grow your financial experience. With a second card, your utilization rate will be lower overall, further helping your credit. You will have an extra hard inquiry in your credit history but still have an excellent score in that category nonetheless. The best thing of all is the card perks and the satisfaction of using them. Don't be scared when applying for your second card. Enjoy the rush and the feeling of building your credit. Let's go have fun!

To look at the different cards per tiers and the best cards per categories, visit LuccianoDiazSkoff.com and reach out to me on Instagram @LuccianoDiazSkoff.

CHAPTER 8.

Hey There, Sexy

———

"Success seems to be connected with action.
Successful people keep moving. They
make mistakes, but they don't quit."

—CONRAD HILTON

So, you are well on your way on your journey to financial freedom, credit cards edition. You have the rules of the game, already have a second card, and some eight to twelve months now in your credit history. Since you already have the hang of it, always paying on time and in full, what's next? Well, your third card, of course!

Ralph Waldo Emerson once said, "The desire of gold is not for gold. It is for the means of freedom and benefit."[49] This means it doesn't matter if it is gold, money, or credit. These, in and of themselves, are not the ultimate goal of wealth. The freedom, opportunities, and life they can provide you are.

---

49   Ralph Waldo Emerson, *The Complete Works*, New York and Boston: Houghton, Mifflin, 1904; Bartleby.com, 2013.

Unlike your first and second cards, where your research was aimed toward getting approved for your first card and then getting a card with some perks or cash back, your third card is a bit different. There is still research to do, ideally for a card that matches either or both of your current cards or to diversify your portfolio of cards.

So, you have more options. Now, with a credit history and two cards already in your report, lenders can see that you have some experience with credit and will be willing to extend some offers previously not accessible to you. They will not necessarily be the offers you want, but most are probably better than what you have.

The fourth card I got was the Chase Freedom Unlimited (CFU), an all-around great card for everyday use. This card had a sign-up bonus (SUB) when I got approved, something neither of the other cards had. It also gives me cash back on categories the other two cards don't cover, for example: travel, dining, and drugstores, and on top of that, a 1.5 percent cash back on every other purchase. It was a no-brainer for me.

Before deciding on this card, I had to first look at my spending habits. I already had gas and food covered. So, what other things did I normally spend on? Well, the supermarket for sure. Getting food in a pandemic when most restaurants are closed is difficult. You can only get it from the markets.

The CFU has five-times the points for the supermarket category, or five points per dollar. Instead of taking out new cards because of the "name" and not actually maximizing them, do you see how my lifestyle instead determines the cards most suitable for me?

Do you know the average number of credit cards your generation has? Take a look at this: Gen Z has an average of 1.4 credit cards, the lowest ownership average. Curiously enough, they have more retail cards for an average of 1.5. Gen X has an average of 3.2 credit cards, very close to the silent generation with 3.0 credit cards. In other words, having three cards puts you close to the national average of four and just shy of Gen X's average. [50]

As for the remaining generations, baby boomers and Gen Y (millennials), I wanted a direct comparison. Baby boomers have the highest credit card average of 3.5, and millennials have just an average of 2.5 cards. It's intriguing that millennials have an average credit card balance of $7,750, compared to baby boomers' average of $6,747. That is a difference of $1,000 with one less credit card. This, then, raises the question: Why? We know that older generations have a better credit score because they have a longer amount of time handling credit. And while they have one more credit card than millennials, they have a big difference in credit limits.[51]

The reason for this $1,000 difference is that millennials worry more than older generations about their credit. More than half of millennials (65 percent) say checking their credit scores helps them make better financial decisions, compared to only 39 percent of baby boomers. At the same time, 78 percent of millennials say their

50   Joe Resendiz, "Credit Card Usage and Ownership Statistics (2019 Report)," ValuePenguin, December 17, 2019.

51   "Millennials Worry More about Credit than Older Adults," CreditCards, August 17, 2020.

credit history directly affects their lives, while only 35 percent of baby boomers agree.[52] As we keep educating ourselves on how to build, grow, and maintain our credit, we inch closer to financial freedom.

Now, before applying to any of those cards, there is something you must do first: check to see if those cards have a pre-qualified link. That will save you the trouble of getting declined. Another helpful measure you can take is to extend your research and search for "data points" on getting approved.

This means you must search on the internet for examples that can help you assess your chances of getting approved. Look at other people's story of why they got either approved or denied for that same card. The more data points, the better. Also, search for examples of the lowest credit score the company has been known to accept for credit cards.

All of this information is helpful on deciding whether you should apply for that card at that moment or choose another card. This is important to know because banks have certain unwritten rules for consumers when applying. An example of this is Chase.

Chase has the famous "five twenty-four rule." This means that they will not approve you for a new card if you have opened five accounts in the last twenty-four months. Yes, you read that right. Although this is strictly for Chase, they do count every new credit card, no matter the bank. So if you received two Banco Popular cards, one Chase

---

52 Megan DeMatteo, "Baby Boomers Have an Average of $25,812 of Debt, Not Including Mortgages—Here's How They Compare to Other Generations," CNBC, December 2, 2020.

card, and two American Express cards in a period of twenty-four months, you will be denied immediately.[53]

In your case, this will be your third card, and so you will not have that problem. To make sure you keep count of how many credit cards you have opened and their time, I urge you to check your credit report. You can do that at AnnualCreditReport.com, a service provided to customers to check their credit and make sure nothing is wrong. This service is available to you for free once a year.

Although you won't be able you view your current credit score, you can monitor your credit health using the report. Chase is not the only bank that has these kinds of rules. Just recently, American Express shared its own set of rules.

One well-known rule with American Express is their "Once-in-a-lifetime" rule.[54] You guessed it—you can only earn the welcome bonus for a specific card once in your life. Thankfully, if you earned the welcome bonus on a personal card, you can still earn the welcome bonus on a business card, and vice versa. But once you get it, it's not coming back, even if you close the account and try to open it again. The reason for this rule is to crack down on credit card churners.

Chase has a similar rule where if you received the welcome bonus once for the card, you cannot earn it again before the twenty-four-month mark. This means that you

---

53   Ethan Steinberg, "The Ultimate Guide to Credit Card Application Restrictions," The Points Guy, May 20, 2020.

54   Brett Holzhauer, "Amex Application Rules—What You Need to Know Before Applying for an Amex Credit Card," ValuePenguin, November 21, 2020.

need to time out your application, not only to space out the hard inquiries in your history, but to earn the highest welcome bonus available.[55]

Likewise, Amex does not approve you for more than one card every five days. The reason for this rule is to prevent credit card fraud if your identity is stolen. To extend the security of its customers, Amex limits the approval of cardholders to two every ninety days. They do not want to extend you too much credit that you will end up in debt.

Lastly, they limit the number of credit cards and charge cards a cardholder can have any given time. That is a maximum of four credit cards and ten charge cards.[56]

While some of us may get to the point of having multiple American Express cards, let's circle back to getting approved for your third card.

Another example that could help you navigate these waters is if you find that a certain bank is known to accept credit card applications of people with a credit score of six hundred eighty and up. When you check your credit score and see you are not quite there yet, you'll want to have a higher credit score before applying. To do that, you can do several things. You can reduce your credit card utilization rate, not take out another card, pay on time and in full, and give it some time before you can reach the desired credit score.

You can work on your credit score to increase your score or choose another card with more flexible requirements.

55   Ethan Steinberg, "The Ultimate Guide to Credit Card Application Restrictions," The Points Guy, May 20, 2020.

56   Brett Holzhauer, "Amex Application Rules—What You Need to Know Before Applying for an Amex Credit Card," ValuePenguin, November 21, 2020.

The decisions you make are yours and will be determined by your situation. These are just examples of real-life situations you might encounter.

I like this quote from Oscar Wilde, it sums up a good credit card user: "A man who pays his bills on time is soon forgotten."[57]

Each credit score is different. Some may need more work than others, and some might just need a hard inquiry to fall off before it can bounce back up. You should sit down and know what is happening with your credit score before making a decision.

Time your application correctly. Make sure to have a low utilization rate, no balance on your cards, and check your credit score on all three credit bureaus with the latest update. Once you have chosen the card that fits your lifestyle, you understand that this will work for you, and you want to keep building your credit history, go apply for it.

If you get accepted, congrats! Keep building your credit score and reaping the rewards. If you did not get accepted, do not despair. Almost all banks have a reconsideration line. Find the phone number of the reconsideration section of the bank, talk with a representative, and explain your situation. This works most of the time since a computer declined your application and not a human.

Once you talk with them and they get to know you better, mention why they are better than the competition. You will most likely get reconsidered and approved. If you do not get approved, do not worry. Keep working on your

---

57 "10 Famous Quotes About Finances & Credit," Credit One Bank, accessed August 19, 2020.

credit score, and with some time you can apply for the card again or apply for an even better one.

Like wine, this is a journey that gets better with time. By the time I applied for my third card four months had passed, and a year since I started building my credit. I got approved with a score of 739, based on my Experian credit score using the VantageScore 3.0.

For reconsideration scripts as well as negotiation tips and letters to remove hard inquires, visit Lucciano-DiazSkoff.com and reach out to me on Instagram @ LuccianoDiazSkoff.

CHAPTER 9.

Business Is Business

———

"The lifeblood of job creation in America is small business, but they can't get access to credit."

—HOWARD SCHULTZ

As a small business owner and player of the credit card game, I wondered if there was a similar product for businesses—a credit card for business. We know that an LLC or an NGO is a separate legal entity with its own social security number (SSN). If it's a business, the SSN is the employer identification number, or EIN, which identifies the business as its own separate entity. Even though you might be the owner, president, or cofounder of the business, it still has an identity of its own. What does this mean? That the business, like you, has an identity that it can use to apply for a credit card. Welcome to business credit cards.

A close friend I am constantly bouncing ideas with is Gautam Sham. Gautam is the owner of the Dream Inn, a beautiful boutique hotel right next to the beach in San Juan,

Puerto Rico. As you enter the architecturally designed guest house lobby, a sense of harmony and tranquility takes over with the settings of a Buddha-inspired colorful koi pond with its soft flow of water and an abstract OM decor. Trust me, it's an amazing place to stay.

One day, hanging out on the rooftop of the hotel with Gautam, I ask him how he managed to keep the business running during the pandemic. "Out of all the things, credit has helped me the most," he said. "Being in the tourism industry, sometimes you have to make big purchases that would be a lot easier to pay in a thirty-, sixty-, or ninety-day period. Having good credit allows me to have a higher credit limit which allows me to make purchases for my business I would normally be unable to do. The pandemic has taken a toll on everyone, but having credit has helped the business stay afloat. Plus, I get points for every purchase."

When looking for your first credit card, having no credit history or credit score and no income, your chances of getting a card are slim. Business credit cards behave similarly, with the only difference being no credit-building card or loan for businesses. You go straight for a business credit card.

For those of you who have a business, this section is for you. The readers that do not have a business can still learn from this too. This is a great section for you to share with your friends and colleagues. A business, legally, is a separate entity, or its own legal entity before the law. Therefore, it can have its own credit cards. Having a credit card for your business has a couple of benefits. They often have the same or better perks than personal credit cards. You can separate business expenses from personal expenses. And some cards only report to commercial credit bureaus.

The following are seven major ways business and personal credit cards differ.

1. How they report to credit bureaus
2. The credit limits
3. Bonus categories
4. Zero percent APR periods
5. Bookkeeping
6. Employee cards
7. Consumer protection[58]

For starters, the way they report: Some cards only report to commercial credit bureaus affecting your business credit. If you are looking to increase your personal credit score, make sure the card you are applying for reports to both personal and commercial credit bureaus. Don't get me wrong, you do not necessarily need a business or EIN to apply. Some issuers encourage you to apply as sole proprietorship for the card. Others do ask for the EIN and utility records. The bureaus and scoring also vary. Personal credit scores range from three hundred to eight hundred fifty, while business credit scores range from zero to one hundred.

CreditCards.com did a study of the small business credit market in 2018. It showed that businesses had less than 4 percent of credit card accounts in circulation (13.9

---

58   Claire Tsosie, "6 Major Differences Between Business and Personal Credit Cards," NerdWallet, June 11, 2020.

million). At the same time, they do quite the heavy lifting, spending $430 billion in credit cards. That is $1 in every $6 spent. Small business credit card purchases are set to reach around $700 billion in 2022.

Furthermore, they found that businesses seeking capital prefer loans and lines to credit cards, although businesses two years old or less were more likely to seek credit cards for capital almost at the same rate as loans and lines of credit. They also found key differentiators between business and consumer credit card use.

Business owners had an average credit score of seven hundred twenty-one versus six hundred seventy-three for consumers. They also had an average of 7.43 open accounts compared to the average of 4.4 for consumers. The most outstanding number of all is the average total credit limit of $56,100 for business owners, more than twice the average of consumer credit limit of $26,900.[59]

A recent report from the SBA shows that small businesses generate 44 percent of US economic activity. Thus, small businesses are the lifeblood of the US economy: They create two-thirds of net new jobs and drive US innovation and competitiveness.[60]

But back to opening a business credit card: Although Experian and Equifax are two of the three bureaus banks report to for personal credit score, they also do business credit score. The difference is while you can access your personal credit scores in Equifax and Experian for free, a business must pay for them.

---

59   "Business Credit Card Statistics," CreditCards, May 6, 2019.

60   Office of Advocacy, "Small Businesses Generate 44 Percent of U.S. Economic Activity," SBA's Office of Advocacy, accessed December 30, 2020.

The third business credit bureau is Dun & Bradstreet, and they are very important. While you can open a business credit with the business EIN, or as a sole proprietor, it will still need a personal guarantee. That is the reason the application also asks for your SSN.

In other words, if the business doesn't pay, you are liable for the debt. How do we separate the business from the person for credit reporting purposes? It depends on the card and bank. Most banks offer business credit cards tied to a personal guarantee because banks believe the owner's personal finances and his company are intertwined. Still, some companies do offer business credit cards with no personal guarantee, like Sam's Club and Shell gas.

✳✳✳

You may have heard this term "DUNS number" if you have a friend or family member who works with or is interested in working with the government. This number also helps establish credit for your business.

To get your DUNS number is fairly simple. Go to DNB. com and follow the steps. The website will guide you through the process. As a heads up, you will need your business name, address, phone number, owner's name, year founded, legal business structure, and number of employees. This is completely free.

Why is having a DUNS number helpful for business credit? Because you want your business credit to be reported to the bureaus, and a DUNS number does just that. It identifies your business for purposes of credit reporting and tracking your financial and payment history.[61] Although not required for businesses to register, this numerical system is widely used around the world.

The DUNS number makes it easier for you to track your credit report, obtain financing, and apply for government contracts, just to name a few. This, in the long run, will also be beneficial for you since your business (hopefully) will continue growing. And so, expanding your credit line with new business credit cards is a smart move.

There is a big difference between business credit and corporate credit. You can get business credit with a sole proprietorship, or an LLC. To build corporate credit, you need vendor accounts, Net 30s, and Paydex score, amongst other things.

Big businesses like Microsoft and Walmart have this type of credit since they are currently and constantly dealing with vendors. For most business owners, a business credit card will get you what you need. They also have higher credit limits.

This brings me to the second major difference: credit limit. Whether you apply as a business or as a sole proprietor, your credit limit should be higher compared to a personal credit card. This is because business credit limits are based on both personal income and business revenue, which are normally higher than your income. And having a high credit limit is never bad.

With business credit cards having such high credit limits, you can expect better categories of perks. While some

---

61   Annie Pilon, "What Is a DUNS Number Used For?," Small Business Trends, July 10, 2020.

still reward you for spending in restaurants and traveling, they start to differ in the bonus categories. The issuers can include rewards in specific categories like the phone bill, online advertising, or office supplies.

Expect your business credit limit to be ten times to one hundred times your personal credit limit. This is helpful in cases where you spend a lot on inventory or services each month. The same way you are smart about choosing the right personal credit card, you should have the same rigorous criteria when choosing a business credit card. The benefits could be great if you know how to use them.

By now, you might be used to or have seen 0 percent APR on personal credit cards ranging anywhere from twelve months all the way up to twenty-one months. Business credit cards aren't so lucky. At most, you can find a 0 percent APR for twelve months or less, varying from six to nine months. Don't worry, you can get another credit card with 0 percent APR for twelve months once the other offer ends.

Business credit cards tend to not offer promotional balance transfers though. If they do, they come with a hefty balance transfer fee. They do not like the business moving the debt to another card and paying it off at a lower interest rate. They also are not that fond of balance transfers and charge transfer fees on top of interest, making it quite hard to pay off your debt in less time.

This major difference is a key benefit of having your business expense and your personal expenses separate. When tax season comes, sitting down and looking at the bank statements and trying to figure out which expense goes where is not a fun way to spend your afternoons.

A business credit card allows you to track every penny spent for the business, making it easier for you to assess the health of your business while also making it easier for the accountant. If the accountant and you are the same person, you have knocked down two birds with one stone.

One other benefit of business credit cards is that you won't always be in the business. Sometimes you might have to run off to some meeting, or the employees need to take care of something when you are not there. With business credit cards you can have extra cards associated with the account for your employees. These are employee credit cards tied to the original business credit card.

In case of an emergency or the employee needs to buy stuff for the job, he or she already has the card. Since it all comes from the same account, you know who spent what where and if he or she is using it as intended.

The last major difference is consumer protection. Even though some business cards do not protect you, most extend their protection as a courtesy to small businesses. Check via phone or online to see if the card you're interested in has these protections.

Key things to know about business credit cards: As personal credit cards improve your credit score, so do business cards improve your business credit. This helps you get a business loan for a project or buy commercial real estate for your headquarters. It can also impact how much you will pay for business insurance. So using your business credit for business transactions instead of your personal credit is beneficial.

As with personal credit, business credit takes time. Opening and using a business credit card is the simplest way to get started. To open a business credit card account, you first need to know if you qualify as a small business. What does that mean? There are a few ways to know. If you have an EIN, are an independent contractor, provide professional services, or sell your service or product, guess what? You are a small business owner.

If you do not have a DUNS number nor an EIN, but still do one of the things mentioned above, you are a sole proprietor. A sole proprietor is the simplest business form under which one can operate a business. Although not a separate legal entity from the owner, it refers to a person who owns the business and is personally responsible for its debts.

These days, it is commonly known as an entrepreneur, where there is no legal distinction between the owner and the business. Examples of this are drop shippers, people who sell things on Amazon, a person who sells homemade goods, or babysitters. It extends to those who teach, tutor, or coach and even those who rent a room or an Airbnb apartment, like myself. So, to all of you reading this selling a product or service on your own, you can apply for a business card.

"Let me remind you that credit is the lifeblood of business, the lifeblood of prices and jobs."[62]

—HERBERT HOOVER

You will need a few things before applying for a business credit card. First, select your card. Chase and American Express have really good cards for all types of businesses. By now, you could already have a relationship

62 Herbert Hoover, *Public Papers of the Presidents of the United States: Herbert Hoover: Containing the Public Messages, Speeches, and Statements of the President, March 4, 1929 to ... March 4, 1933* (Washington, D.C.: Office of the Federal Register, National Archives and Records Services, General Services Administration, 1974). 467

with one or both banks if you have one of their personal credit cards. Don't worry if you don't. You can check their products on their website or on your portal if you have an account with them.

As we have talked about choosing the card that fits your lifestyle, choose the card that fits your business. This card will be the stepping-stone to building business credit. A personal favorite of mine is the Costco Business credit card. It has the same perks and cash back as the personal card.

I find everything for my business at Costco. Sheets, towels, printer tint, cleaning products, even the snacks I leave for my guests. You do need a Costco membership to get one. Once you have selected the card, get the information in order and start the application process.

These are the most common questions you will find in most business credit card applications:

- Legal business name: If you have one, write it down. If you do not, you can use your own name.

- Business name: It looks the same, but it isn't. In this case, it would be your business name again or your name if you are the sole proprietor.

- Business address: This would be the business address when operating an independent business, or it could be your home address.

- Business structure: In the type of business or company structure, you must choose between corporation, partnership, or sole proprietor.

- Business category: In the business category, you will select from a wide range of business categories.

Remember to always select the category that best describes your business.

- Identification number: To provide the federal tax ID number means your employee identification number if you are a business or your social security number as sole proprietor.

- Years in Business: The following is straight forward: years in business and annual business revenue.

- Business profit: For this section, you will report the net profit of your business.

- Number of employees: And last in your business information is how many employees you have. If you are applying as a sole proprietor, you are the only employee.

After you are done with this section, it will prompt you to fill out your personal information. This is because your credit score is a determining factor in reviewing your credit worthiness for your business. Although every business card uses your credit score to determine your eligibility for a business credit card, not all report to the personal credit bureaus, thus not affecting your personal credit.

They will need your personal credit score in order to apply for a business credit card. The reason for this is because the business has no credit the bank can use to evaluate your application. They also need a personal guarantee in case the business does not pay its debt.

Before hitting send, review your answers and make sure they are correct and accurate. You will know in the moment if you are accepted. If you do not, the bank will reach out to you; they will probably want to get to know your business.

Congrats! You are off to building your business credit!

I'd like to finish this chapter with a small excerpt from a Graham Stephan interview in the *Bigger Pockets* podcast. Graham is asked, "What would you tell your staff to do today if they got some really good deals?" To which he answers, "Well, the thing is, back then I was buying these deals [with] cash because I didn't have a credit card. I didn't have any credit whatsoever. And if I simply had a credit card, I could have financed all of them. I could have put even like 30 percent down, 40 percent down, whatever, and financed them."[63]

Graham says that in his early days he missed a couple of great deals because he did not have a credit card, a tool that would have let him finance the purchase.

So, all you entrepreneurs and business owners should build your personal credit to build your business credit. Business credit helps you finance and expand your operation. It will also let you fulfill other financial needs while changing people's lives.

For more statistics on business credit and credit cards and to learn how to start business and corporate credit, visit LuccianoDiazSkoff.com and reach out to me on Instagram @LuccianoDiazSkoff.

---

63 "How to Become a Millionaire Through Real Estate by Age 26," How to Become a Millionaire Through Real Estate by Age 26, *BiggerPockets Real Estate* Podcast, December 26, 2020.

CHAPTER 10.

Churn, Baby, Churn

——

*"Learn from the mistakes of others. You can't
live long enough to make them all yourself."*

—ELEANOR ROOSEVELT

As you wait for your third card to arrive, you start to plan
out how you would use the welcome bonus. You jump on
the internet and search for "maximizing points on my
card" or "earn welcome bonus faster." As you dive in,
you start to see how others have gotten their welcome or
sign-up bonus in a couple of days. You start planning out
the trips with the points, how many points you need, and
the cards that will help you get there. As you finish building your *points machine* for free flights, you see there is
one card you did not include there: your first card.

In a couple of months, you lost interest in it. Maybe you
do not use your card anymore because you "churned" it
completely. Or you are just merely "meh" about it and are
thinking about closing your account. It could also be that

you just got bored with your first card. All those feelings are normal. Then you think, Hmm, if I'm not using the card as much, let me just close it. I have been there, and let me tell you this: it doesn't actually make sense to close the account. At least, not those accounts that have the most weight in your credit score, which are usually the ones that you don't use and store away in your drawer.

You see, just because you used up all the sign-up bonuses of your card or your lifestyle changed and your everyday card doesn't suit you now, it is not a reason to close the accounts. Those accounts, believe it or not, make up your credit history, the same credit history that banks, credit unions, auto dealers, and beyond see before offering you a product.

You might come across posts on Facebook or Instagram about the seventy-four cards this one person has or the fifteen of the same card the other person has. And you'd see the photos of the cards stacked together and everyone liking the post. Then you wonder, What is this person doing? Why so many cards? Does he need them all? Is he in debt? It doesn't make sense.

While scrolling the post you see comments like, "Wow, you should have around one million miles with so many cards." And another person saying, "Do you use them all?" Then, you may see a comment about churning the cards because he travels all the time; how he opens a card, uses the welcome bonus, and closes it the next week. You say to yourself, "This doesn't make sense." Well, that is credit card churning, and it's a huge problem for banks.

What is credit card churning? Great question. Some of you might get two or three cards in your lifetime, and they will most likely be the only cards you ever get. But, because you are reading this, by now you know that having two or three cards is not your goal. Your goal is to start achieving your financial freedom by maximizing the credit card perks. You can do this actively, or passively.

Credit card churning is the act of applying and opening new credit card accounts, hitting those sign-up bonuses in the shortest time period, and then closing the account.[64] You then keep repeating the process of opening and closing the same credit card repeatedly to get the welcome bonus every time. The welcome bonus typically includes cash back or points redeemable for flights. The points cards are where the money is. You do this so many times that you see the points in your account multiply so fast and you can technically fly for free all year long. Friends, beware—most companies have cracked down on credit card churners, shutting down all of their accounts plus not allowing them to apply for and open the same credit card inside a twelve- to twenty-four-month period. It's serious.

I don't do this because I *want* to keep a good relationship with my banks. I love the customer service on the Amex Platinum. I love all the benefits Chase offers. And even though I rarely use my Banco Popular card, I'll do business with them in the future.

You can churn your cards passively or actively. A passive churner is someone not actively looking for new cards and applying to get the bonus in the shortest time

---

64   Amanda Dixon, "The Pros and Cons of Credit Card Churning," SmartAsset, July 9, 2018.

possible. Instead, every six months or so, they get a new credit card with the bonus.

On the other hand, those who are actively churning cards are very aggressive, getting cards every week. There are different fashions of doing this. The most basic way is getting a card with a high welcome bonus. Those usually have an annual fee. Then, they hit that minimum spend, use the card to the fullest, and just when the annual fee is about due, close the card, wait a couple of weeks, and do it all over again.

This evolved to what is called an app-o-rama, applying to three or more cards the same day to get ahead of the system.[65] This way, not all hard inquiries would show at the same time, increasing their chance of getting accepted. This could also be done by applying to different cards of the same bank. The banks would use one hard inquiry to approve you for three or four cards the same day. Once that is done, you do it all over again in three months.

Banks took notice and have since established rules, written and unwritten, to fight churners. We've discussed some of those rules like Chase's five twenty-four rule, where you would instantly be denied if you have opened five or more cards in the past twenty-four months. And the Amex five ninety rule, where you can apply for a new credit card in a five-day period and have two new cards in the last ninety days. Recently, there have been many account shutdowns for people bending the rules.

Shutdowns happen primarily when you go against the terms and conditions or do something they explicitly

---

65 Jeffrey Brownson, "What Is Credit Card Churning?" *Forbes Magazine*, December 8, 2020.

said you cannot do. Most commonly are manufactured spending (we'll talk about this in a bit) and brokering of points or rewards. Simply put, it is the selling, buying, or trading of reward points and miles between accounts. This is always against the terms and conditions.

Another reason you might get your account shutdown is for risky behavior. For example, you may have too many applications in too little time, too much credit extended, and in a similar manner, spending that does not match your income. Lastly, tying it all together, you're cycling your limits pretty fast and spending your limit too quickly. This means maxing out your card, paying it off completely, and doing it all over again in a short period.

Another rule against churners is Amex's lifetime rule. You can only get the welcome bonus once in your lifetime. Companies have these sign-up bonuses because they want more customers signing up for their cards. As an active churner, you want to hit those welcome bonuses as fast as possible to close the card and apply for another.

Active churners are also commonly known as "travel hackers." For example, Phillip travels to and from Puerto Rico every two weeks. His company gave him the option of using a company card to charge everything to it or using his personal cards and getting the reimbursement. Guess which one Phillip chose? Exactly, he chose the latter. Why? Because instead of accruing the points on the company card, which the company then uses for its own trips, he chose to get those same points on his own card. Isn't that great? Since his company reimburses his travels to and from Puerto Rico, company meals and dinners, lodging, and ridesharing, you can imagine how many points he has racked up on his card. He can then use those same points to travel for free around the world, pay for hotels, rent cars, get cash-back, and more. By having his trips paid for, he can open and close a card every four months or so. Yet, he is not a travel hacker.

A travel hacker is someone who churns fifteen or more cards a year just for the benefits. As a churner, you'd typically close cards that have an annual fee, closing them before they are due. And instead of closing other cards with no annual fee, they ask for a product change. A product change is when the bank changes your current credit card for a new credit card product. By doing this, the banks just change the card but keep the account open. The benefit of asking for a product change is you do not close your current account and still benefit from the welcome bonus of the new card.

The goal behind all of this is to have enough points in your account to buy the plane tickets and the hotel rooms at a fraction of the price. Because you have the points, it does not mean it is free. Remember that you had to spend money to get the welcome bonus. But what you would have otherwise spent to get the points is still a lot more if it were not for the welcome bonus. Hence, this is a very easy decision.

Another fashion of credit card churning is buying prepaid cards and using them to pay the balance. This is called manufactured spending.[66] The goal of a churner is to hit the welcome bonus as soon as possible to close the card and get on to the next welcome bonus. It doesn't matter

---

66   Nick Reyes, "Manufactured Spending Complete Guide," December 16, 2020.

what you spend the money on, as long as you hit the goal and pay it all back. This is where prepaid cards come to close the loop. Prepaid cards have a preset amount of money you can put in. Some even let you add a bit more.

Let's say you have to spend $1,000 to hit the goal and get the welcome bonus. Well, instead of going out to dinner every day, buy ten $100 prepaid cards. That simple. Do not buy it all at once, because you do not want it to be obvious. You spread enough to buy them and pay them back. The money-move with prepaid cards is that you withdraw the money from the card to pay the balance you owe. In other words, you are using the bank's money to pay for the welcome bonus.

As you can guess, banks do not like that at all. This kind of churning is very risky, since banks can detect what you are doing, freeze your account, and take all the points away. Oh yes, they can. And they also add a mark on your name, so they are careful the next time you apply for any of their cards. The police can put you on watch because this is similar to money laundering even though it is a loophole in the system.

Be warned: "Some churners are able to get lots of freebies multiple times a year, just by using the right credit cards. But this strategy isn't right for everyone."[67] I agree with my friends at NerdWallet—this is not for everyone and has some risks. The following are some tips to help you churn your cards safely. When shopping for a new card, not every website has the same offers. Look around at a couple of sites and see which one has the highest offer. Websites like CreditCards.com offer pre-qualify links.

---

67 Erin Hurd, "Should I Try Credit Card Churning?," NerdWallet, July 29, 2020.

Also, check your emails or accounts to see what they might have for you. Apps like NerdWallet routinely show you cards you might be eligible for (but most are paid advertisements). Why do people close the account after churning the card? We all hate them: fees. Most of the cards that have a ridiculous offer or sign-up bonus come with an annual fee. Instead of paying the fee, most people choose to close the account and forget about them. Where you normally find the terms and conditions of the card is where you can find the fees.

American Express, for example, only lets you earn the bonus for a specific card. This means that you will be unable to earn the bonus for the same card in the future. Chase has a limit for everyone trying to get a new Chase card, the five twenty-four rule.[68] You cannot have opened five or more personal credit cards in the last twenty-four months. Although the rule only applies when applying to Chase issued cards, the five credit card count includes cards from all banks. In other words, be savvy when applying to Chase.

Opening too many cards, in a very short period, can also be hazardous for your credit score. The fees associated with your cards can go unnoticed if you are not keeping track of how many cards you have opened nor keeping tabs on your spending. That is extremely hurtful for your credit score. Opening numerous credit cards in a short period can raise lenders' concern for you, viewing your recent credit applications as a sign of financial trouble and denying your applications. Not keeping track of your

---

68   Richard Kerr, "The Ultimate Guide to Chase's 5/24 Rule," The Points Guy, May 1, 2020.

applications and spending also leads you to carry a balance on your cards, and we all know the result of that.

My last tip is to keep a record of your churning. Write down the credit card, the date you opened it, the target bonus date, annual fee date (if any), the bonus amount, spending requirements, bonus last date, your balance, and your progress. Keep tabs for all of this, and you will be just fine. One last thing: If you do not have the money to meet the bonus requirements by the date, do not go through all the trouble of applying for it and then having the dissatisfaction of not achieving the offer.

With that feeling comes the downsides and risks of credit card churning. First, by opening a ton of credit cards, your credit score will take a massive hit. It will not tank your score, but you will definitely see the difference. You won't see much difference if you have an extensive credit history, like if your oldest account is ten years old and you have seven years of average credit history. On the other hand, watch out if you have less than three years and less than five cards. This will hurt.

Second: There is a risk of opening a ton of credit cards and not keeping up with the payments. It happens, y'all. You forget to pay the balance on your card. Imagine opening up one card per week for two months just for the sign-up bonus. Then, you cannot keep track of your cards and start missing payments on eight cards. Figure out what that would look like. Your credit score is already down due to all the hard inquiries, and you are dragging it even farther down by not paying on time. It will take you some time to get back up to the seven hundred forty-plus credit score. A piece of advice:

"You want 21 percent risk free? Pay off your credit cards."[69]

—ANDREW TOBIAS.

Third: You could weaken your credit age by opening a ton of credit cards and closing them. Even though the cards have not been on your credit history for enough time to make an impact, specifically on your credit history, closing them will affect your total age of credit (that is why people close them before the first month after they're opened). The hardest impact is in your utilization rate. If you choose to close cards with an outgoing balance, your credit card utilization rate will go up. Take it from the experts at NerdWallet: "Closing your credit cards can ding you on two fronts: your credit utilization and your average age of accounts—both of which factor into your credit scores."[70]

For example: You have two cards, both with a $1,000 credit limit. Card A has a $0 balance, and card B has a $1,000 balance. Right now, your utilization rate is at 50 percent (total balance divided by credit limit). If you close one, you now have $1,000 of credit balance on a $1,000 credit limit, getting you to a 100 percent utilization rate. We both know that is not good.

Credit card churning has its advantages and disadvantages. You can get five hundred thousand points in a matter of months as well as lose all your points in a matter of days. It's no fun waking up to an email saying you have lost all your points, all your accounts are closed, and the bank doesn't want you. And to be clear, the act of closing

---

69   Andrew Tobias, "Chapter Checklist Financial Needs What About a Loan," *American Way*, November 1982.

70   Steve Bucci, "How Closed Account Affects Credit Score," CreditCards.com, May 28, 2020.

a credit card has no substantial effect on your credit score *per se*. It is everything that it takes away from your report. We'll discuss more on this in the next chapter.

As you keep building your credit and enjoying your journey, the game will get easier to play. You will get the hang of it and even get cocky with it too, just to try it out. You might get bored with a card pretty quickly and start looking for the next welcome bonus. In the process, tips and tricks to hit the welcome bonus faster will start appearing. Getting cards every three months and showing them off sounds sexy. I hope that with what you have learned here, you make the right decision and that you will use the cards as a tool to build your financial freedom.

To get a guide on how to keep up with sign up bonuses, annual fees, and spending, visit me at LuccianoDiazSkoff. com and reach out on Instagram @LuccianoDiazSkoff.

CHAPTER 11.

Don't Press Cancel

———

"By failing to prepare, you are preparing to fail."

—BENJAMIN FRANKLIN

Throughout this book, we've learned that keeping our cards open for the longest amount of time is key to building credit. Sometimes, that is not possible. Economic hardship, a pandemic, and overall uncertainty are all reasons we might start pondering what to do with our credit cards.

By this chapter, you should have at least three cards in your wallet, maybe four if you took out two in the beginning. Also by now, we know that credit cards can save our lives in difficult times. They helped my dad start his business. They've helped people get by these past few months.

In case you still distrust credit cards, do not close the ones you started with. Those three or four cards in your wallet are the ones building your credit for the future. They are laying the foundation in your credit report to support more cards, more loans, and however many mortgages you want. Also, in a worst-case scenario, they will help you bounce back from a bankruptcy.

Right now, it is important to nurture your credit score. Avoid adding any negative items on your credit report. Do the right things at the right time. Building your credit for your first two or three years is the most important thing. Nothing else matters. And you will see why.

"If a person established good credit, the impact of card closure should be minimal and short-lived," says Christina Goethe, former spokeswoman for FICO, the provider of the most commonly used credit score.[71]

Let's imagine you are far ahead in your credit card game. As you start accumulating cards, you will see that some of your cards start to lose their value. This is due to a couple of reasons. Most of the time, you start mixing and matching cards to max out their points and perks, switching cards out from your daily carry for better cards with better perks.

Another common thing that starts happening is that you no longer take full advantage of the cards with a high annual fee. Maybe your lifestyle changed. You changed to a job that no longer supports you using your cards, you got married and your priorities changed, or you want to start growing roots in a place instead of flying around. That is all fine. As long as you handle your cards accordingly, everything will be all right.

Although I am against closing cards, I understand you might sometimes need to. You will learn how to do it without damaging your credit score.

---

71 Fred O. Williams, "How to Cancel a Credit Card Without Hurting Your Credit Score," CreditCards.com, December 10, 2020.

A huge misconception is that closing accounts hurts your credit score. It does, but not necessarily in the way you have heard. Closing an account will not affect your credit history in the immediate future. As credit expert John Ulzheimer, formerly from Fico and Equifax, says, "As long as the credit card remains on your report, you will still get the value of the age of the account in both the FICO and VantageScore branding credit scoring models. The only way to lose the value of the age of the card is if it's removed from your reports."[72]

Closed accounts, like derogatory marks, stay on your credit history between seven and ten years. In other words, once you close an account and do not write to bureaus to get it removed before the time, you still have seven to ten years of that account impacting your credit history.[73]

Why seven to ten years? It depends. Is it a positive closed account, or a negative closed account? If you missed a payment, had a collection in that account, or it was delinquent before closing your account, the account with all the negative effects stays in your report for seven years.

Otherwise, a positive closed account, which means you never missed a payment and it was healthy, stays on your credit history for ten years. It may not have the same impact as an opened account, but it is still a positive thing.

Before I venture on how to close a credit card, as a responsible credit card user, I will issue your warnings

---

72   Michelle L. Black, "The Safe Way to Cancel a Credit Card," Investopedia, May 20, 2020.

73   John S Kiernan, "Derogatory Credit: What It Means & How To Avoid It," WalletHub, February 21, 2016.

first. At the same time, I will provide you with examples of when it makes sense to close the card and when it doesn't and the things you can do instead of closing the card. Let's start.

As soon as you close your card, you will have fewer lines of credit, thus lowering the amount of credit available to you, and if you are not careful this will ultimately increase your credit card utilization rate. And that is just as soon as the next credit score update.

Be aware that both of those things can negatively impact your credit score. A reason you might have for closing a card is high fees and low rewards. You feel that the annual fees you are paying for your card and the rewards you are getting back are not necessarily worth it. I understand why you'd want to close the card.

Another reason might be that the card has a high interest rate and you need to carry a balance. That card is definitely one you should stop using. If you want to spend less and know you will not make the most out of the rewards, this might be another reason to cancel the card.

I should give you a heads up when canceling a card: choose the right time to do it. Do not close a card when you are planning on getting another credit card or buying a car or getting a house.

Remember, closing a card drops your credit score a few points for a couple of months, and those same points could determine whether you can get the car loan or mortgage. Always have this in mind.

It is über important to close the accounts when there is a separation or divorce or when the temptation to use the cards is too high. If you fall out of love with your partner and you have a joint account with them, close it without hesitation. Having a joint account means that both of you are liable to whatever happens. And if your partner wants to screw you over, they might start charging things to that account, leaving you with 100 percent of the responsibility for it. So, closing that account might save you numerous problems and debt. Yes, I know this sounds crazy, but this does happen.

Just like a joint account, having too much of an urge to use the credit card is bad for you. Although you have learned in this book the three rules to avoid any fees or debt, sometimes people might get carried away with the status or perks of the card. If removing the cards from your wallet does not work for you, try cutting it with scissors or hiding it. If that still doesn't work, it is better to lower your credit limit or even cancel it.

Now you know the times you might think of canceling a credit card. Before you do that, I suggest a couple of things to avoid canceling them. First, if the card has an annual fee, call the bank and ask them to waive the fee for you. Sometimes this works, sometimes it doesn't. It comes down to how well you sell it to the bank that you are a great loyal customer and are thinking of closing the card.

If that is not possible or you see that card is not worth it for you, ask the bank to downgrade the product or convert your current product to one with no fee. This is called a product change. This is easier for the banks to do, so you might have better luck trying it.

But let's say you gave those two options a chance and they didn't work. If you are simply focused on closing the card, stop before pulling the trigger. There are three circumstances in which I urge you not to do it.

First, it is the account with the oldest history in your credit score. We all know what happens if you close your oldest opened account, right? Your credit score with take a huge hit and plummet quite a few points.

Secondly, your credit mix may not be that mixed or you do not have enough open accounts. When your credit history is thin, closing an account might make it harder to get more credit products in the future.

Lastly, if the only reason you are canceling the card is because you do not use it and its useful life ended quite a while ago, then instead of closing it down, buy a bottle of water once a year with it and keep it open. It will serve you better leaving it open than closing it.

At last, here is how to close a credit card safely. First, see if you have any unused points in your account and ask what happens to them when you close the account. Some banks erase your points—what a tragedy—while others leave your points in the account available for you to use. In both cases, ask the bank the points' expiring date, if any.

Once you are sure how to handle your points, pay off any outstanding balance you have. At the very least try to minimize your balance as much as possible. Doing this will help you avoid the surprise of having a higher utilization rate when you cancel the card. Call and ask the bank to make sure you have no balance in the account and there are no pending payments on it.

After you know your points are safe and you owe nothing to the bank, send them a letter telling them to cancel the account. In it, ask them to mail you back the confirmation of your $0 balance on the account and confirmation of closed account status. The confirmation letter might help you in the future if there is an error in your credit history. This is called a closed by request note. Banks automatically do this by default, so just make sure it shows up. Also, you would like to have this note in your credit history to show anyone looking at your report that *you* wanted to close the account, not that it was closed by the bank for not paying on time or being irresponsible with your credit.

Lastly, check your report with the three credit bureaus one to two months after you closed the account. If you find any error, dispute it. All will be fine.

Finally, congrats! You have successfully closed your account.

"If repairing one's credit is as easy as sending some dispute letters to the credit bureaus then why doesn't everyone have good credit?"[74]

One exception to the rules of closing a credit card is if you are an expert in the credit game. Since you have been playing the game for some years, you will have the experience and expertise to not make mistakes. Once you have a solid credit profile with some fifteen-something cards on record, you will start to open and close key cards just for the benefits. An example of this is closing a Chase card to get the bonus again. Chase lets you earn the bonus on the same card as long as you did not earn it in the past twenty-four months.

---

74   Emily Morgan, "Credit Repair - DIY vs Professional Help," Fit My Money, November 24, 2020.

You might have so many cards one day and cards that have better perks than others that instead of closing the account, you store them in your drawer and never use them again. Be aware of this: The bank or credit issuer might close your account if it has been inactive.

No standard timeframe exists for when a card issuer will decide to close an account due to inactivity, although some cards might revoke any unredeemed points, miles, or cash back you saved on your card if you do not use it at all. They usually do that after twelve months of inactivity. In some instances, credit card issuers have closed accounts after six months of inactivity.

The best way to avoid getting an account closed is using it every so often, at least once or twice a year. Having an account closed will hurt your credit score by shortening the amount of time you have had an account opened, therefore hurting your credit history. Not using your card is good for your credit score, 0 percent utilization rate, and so on and so forth. And, if you plan to store your card and not use it for a while, at least make sure there is no balance or debt on it, because it will continue accumulating interest.

The more credit lines you have and the more credit mix in your credit history, the higher your credit score. This is the reason I do not like closing credit card accounts. I'd rather go through the trouble of using it once a year to avoid closing it.

If you need to close one, remember to pay off your balance and lower your credit card utilization rate before calling it quits. Doing this saves you the trouble of having a high utilization rate, which then lowers your credit score. Do not close credit cards if you plan on buying a car, getting another card, or buying a house.

As I mentioned in the last chapter, the act of closing an account does not affect your credit score. When you close an account, you shorten or lower the age of credit, you might increase your utilization rate, and you have one closed account more than before. Those are the things that affect your credit directly.

Leave your credit alone for some time before taking action. It will help your credit score and your chances of getting better rates. Remember, closing accounts safely only impacts your credit score negatively for a couple of months. You will be back on your feet in no time.

This is a quick checklist in order to close a credit card:

1. Redeem any points or rewards left before you call to close.

2. If possible, lower your balances to $0 or as much as possible.

3. Call your credit card issuer to confirm there is no balance and close the account.

4. Mail a certified letter to your card issuer to close the account. In it, ask that a letter confirming your $0 balance and closed account status be mailed to you in return.

5. Check your three credit reports one to two months after cancellation to make sure that the account reports it was closed by the cardholder and that your balance is $0.

6. Dispute any incorrect information on your reports with the three credit bureaus. [75]

---

75   Michelle L. Black, "The Safe Way to Cancel a Credit Card," Investopedia, May 20, 2020.

Read the fine print, plan your applications, and follow the rules. Keep enjoying your cards and their benefits. Share with your friends and family how you mastered the credit card game. Teach them how they can master it too. Credit cards are a tool available to everyone. Use it to start your journey to financial freedom.

For this and more useful checklists, visit me at LuccianoDiazSkoff.com and reach out on Instagram @LuccianoDiazSkoff.

CHAPTER 12.

Things Have Changed

—

"Cumulatively small decisions, choices, actions, make a very big difference."

—JANE GOODALL

One morning, my brother, Gustavo, sent me a screenshot of his credit score saying, "I am going to apply for a card. It's a business credit card, so I should be approved, right?" Not exactly, brother. I quickly called him and told him to stop.

My brother is the owner at JoinBased.com, an online technology platform that connects entrepreneurs to ecosystems around Latin America and the Caribbean. JoinBased builds and prints digital magazines and publications for digital nomads.

Gustavo wanted to get a business credit card to fulfill bulk print orders whenever pre-sales are not enough. And he was eager to do it when he saw his credit score jumped seventy-four points to seven hundred forty-six.

I asked him if he had checked other credit monitoring platforms, just to be sure. He said no. When he opened Credit Karma, his eyes opened wide. He had a six hundred ninety and a seven hundred twenty, not exactly the scores he was expecting.

Later that day, we met for a work session and he asked me about his credit. He was worried because one app showed that his credit increased by seventy-four points, while the other showed it had decreased by two points. First, I said, "When was the last time you checked your credit?" "I don't know, maybe a month ago or so?" He had no idea what was happening with his credit. The work session turned into a credit session, going over his complete credit report and setting goals to apply for new cards.

The Experian website says:

> You can check your credit score whenever you want, and there are ways to check several versions of your credit scores for free. Checking your credit will never hurt your scores. Even if you can check your score for free at any time, however, you don't necessarily need to check it every day—especially if you have a credit monitoring service that will notify you of suspicious changes.[76]

A healthy practice is to sit down twice a month and go over your credit report, ideally while you take care of your personal finances. You can use free apps, like Credit Karma and NerdWallet, or paid apps, like myFICO and

---

76 Louis DeNicola, "How Often Should I Check My Credit Score?" Experian, December 9, 2020.

Smartcredit. I prefer myFICO. It is the most accurate consumer app to check your credit. For extra credit monitoring, check your credit cards using FICO's free credit score service. Those scores will be accurate to the date of reporting.

The practice of monitoring your credit is important for various things. First, you get excited watching your credit score go up, or if it goes down, you now know why. Secondly, it helps you to plan ahead. If you are looking to buy a house or a car, knowing exactly when helps you get the better offer. Lastly, it helps in making sure everything is in its place, that the information on your report is correct, and nothing weird or unknown is in your credit report. If you see something, you know what to do.

When monitoring your credit health, you might notice something changed in your credit score—not the usual drop or increase of your score, but an increase in your credit card utilization rate. You wonder why; maybe you used your card more than you should have, or it got misplaced and someone is using it.

As you scroll through your favorite credit score monitoring app, you see a change in the total amount of credit available to you. Your credit limit on a card was lowered automatically, and this comes as a surprise since you did not ask for it, nor did your bank inform you of the change.

Suddenly you realize this is the reason your utilization rate increased. Now you are sitting there, trying to understand what happened. "Why did my credit limit decrease? Why did I not know about this? Can the banks decrease my limit?"

The short answer to the last question is, yes. It is relatively uncommon for banks to lower your credit limit, but it does happen.

Take, for example, the 2020 pandemic: It not only affected the health and businesses of the people, but their finances took a toll too. Card issuers throughout the world considered lowering the credit limits of their cardholders to reduce the risks of exposure during an economic downturn or uncertainty.

In other words, banks lower their customer credit lines to mitigate the risk of defaults and debt associated with the period. A recession or a pandemic (in this case, both) were reasons for the banks to lower your credit limit. Some banks even went further by not accepting new credit card applications for personal or business use.

As the pandemic expanded all through the world, businesses closed, people lost their jobs, and the economy stopped for a brief moment. What happens when you stop making money and have to pay your bills? You either don't pay them and default, disappear, or find a way to pay them.

Most people did just that. Only this time, instead of opening a credit card account to pay the bills, they used the government's money to do that. And how much did US consumers pay down? A total of $68.7 billion.[77] Yep, instead of using the money the government gave them to buy things, they chose to pay down their debt.

---

77 Mish, "Consumer Credit Declines an Amazing $68.7 Billion," Mish Talk, June 5, 2020.

Even though most Americans chose to pay down their debt, banks could still lower your credit limit for any of the following reasons: you stopped using the card, your credit score dropped, your identity was stolen, or there was an error in your credit report.[78] Other reasons include you changed your spending habits, you're behind in your payments or missed a payment, or you've gone over a 50 percent utilization rate. I have taught you the tools and knowledge so you can bounce back from any of these situations.

Any of those scenarios can be reasons for banks to lower your credit limit without your knowledge. They can go through with this because no law prohibits the bank from doing this. Although Congress passed the CARD act, only one provision protects you from the credit limit decrease: if that action accrues fees in your balance.[79]

But since banks wave those fees to avoid penalty, usually credit cardholders hold the short end of the stick. Know that if the bank lowering your credit forces you to accrue fees, they have to, by law, send you a forty-five-day notice of your credit limit lowering. They also cannot charge you an over-the-limit fee forty-five days after your limit is changed. All of those reasons make you look like a risky borrower, and banks do not like that.

What do you do if you find yourself in this situation? First, call your credit card company to understand the

78   Jennifer Nelson, "A Drop in Your Card's Credit Limit Is Bad News for Your Credit Score—Here Are 8 Reasons It Could Happen, and What You Can Do to Fix It," *Business Insider*, March 16, 2020.

79   Brady Porche, "Credit Card Limit Decreased? Why It Happens, and What to Do about It," CreditCards.com, August 28, 2020.

change. Based on that knowledge, you can take corrective action to restore your previous credit limit.[80]

If the reason is that your spending habits changed, explain the situation you are in and how "life happened" that led you to this spending behavior. And if this behavior is tied to a high balance, share your plan on paying off your balance. You can also reduce your debt to lower your credit card utilization rate, another reason for them to lower your limit, or open a new credit card account.

Lastly, if the reason for the action is your low usage, you can commit to using your credit card more. Both will benefit you in the long run. As much as you can, keep your limits as high as possible. It will help with your credit card utilization rate as well as your credit score.

Other than your usual ups and downs of your credit score, don't be too worried about it. I was one that when I started playing the game and writing about it, I would check all my credit apps several times a day. The scores didn't change much day after day. It only mattered when the reports came in from the bureaus or when one app would show an estimate of my score for the past week based on my utilization rate. Sometimes I found discrepancies in the apps because they weren't up to date with the same information. With time, I learned that checking it every day did not change a thing. But keeping my utilization rate down, paying in full, on time, every time, and being smart about using my card did have a significant impact.

You'll get used to watching your score go up and down month by month. As long as everything looks good, you

---

80   John Egan, "What to Do If Your Credit Limit Decreases," Experian, April 23, 2020.

know why there is a high utilization rate, and where the new credit line came from, it's all good. Once you see something that does not make sense, do your research first before taking any action.

One night, after a whole day moving equipment from one apartment to another, I grabbed a drink with my colleague Christian López. Our go-to drink is the *Cuba Libre*, or "*un Cubita.*" And between us, we'd rather have it with Don Q rum. (Sorry, Bacardi.) Christian tells me he discovered on his credit history that he had a seventeen-year-old card, half his age. In other words, the card was opened with his name, supposedly, when he was seventeen years old.

Strangely, he does not have any recollection of doing that whatsoever. Upon further inspection, he recognizes the store: Walmart. We traced when Walmart opened in Puerto Rico, then in his community, and checked the opening date of the card. It all cleared out. The weirdest thing of all is that the person who opened that card seventeen years ago is still using it.

We figured it couldn't be a stranger, nor an identity theft. Which thief would pay, every time without missing a month, for seventeen years? To give you perspective, the card had 204 on-time payments. That is crazy! Out of the 204 times the person could have missed a payment, he or she never did.

Both of us were baffled after figuring out what happened and concluded that his mother probably added him as an authorized user on her card and has been using it ever since. Again, what thief takes out a card on someone else's name and does not miss a payment in seventeen years?

The next day, Christian talked to his mom and calls me. "Bro, I couldn't resist, and I asked my mom if she knew something about the card. Could you believe it was her who took out the card on my name seventeen years ago?" I responded, "Mystery solved. And good for her, she did you a solid. That card has actually built up your credit for the past seventeen years. That is why you get so many offers." Then, the most amazing thing happened. He told me, "You know what my mom said? That card is actually the card that has helped the family in the worst of times." This is the beauty of credit cards.

As you know, I used to check my credit score every day when I started this journey—a couple of times a day, in fact. Nowadays, I check it when I pay my card or when prepping for an application. You know, to keep everything in order and make sure there are no changes.

Before you start checking your credit report, let me tell you what you will find. When checking your credit score through the bank's portal, you will see one score from either of the three bureaus. But not all three show the same score. For example, Chase reports your score from Experian using VantageScore 3.0. American Express uses VantageScore 3.0 too, but to report from TransUnion. And Discover also uses your TransUnion score to report your score using the FICO model.

So, you have three different banks using three different credit scores with two different models. What about third-party apps? They aren't so different. Credit Karma shows your TransUnion and Equifax credit score using the VantageScore 3.0 model, while myFICO shows you your Experian, Equifax, and TransUnion credit score using their model. You're probably saying right now, "What the heck? Which number should I look at then?" The short answer is, all of them.

You should check all of them to make sure there are no changes on your credit report. When doing that, you will notice that not all have the same thing reported—specifically, your hard inquiries. Even though banks check your credit score from all three credit bureaus, most of them pull your report from Experian. Aside from the two scoring models (VantageScore 3.0 and FICO), this is one of the reasons your credit scores are not always the same. Banks largely do a hard pull from one credit bureau.

Let's use my credit report from a while back. It says I have eight hard inquiries. You know the only time a bank pulled my report from all three bureaus? When I was buying a house. That was the only time. American Express, Discover, and the SBA used only my Experian report. Chase has been the only bank so far that has pulled my Experian report as well as my TransUnion report.

Now you're asking, "But Lucciano, how do I check my credit report for that?" Let me show you.

First, you now know that apps like Credit Karma and NerdWallet provide you with educational scores. You can use them to have an idea of where you are. You can find a more accurate score on your scorecard from the bank you have a credit card with. They update once a month and only show you one score. To see all three scores and download your monthly credit report, use myFICO. This has been my favorite credit monitoring tool for a while.

When you open any credit scorecard, the first thing you will see is a number. That is your credit score. And somewhere close to your credit score is the date when it was last updated. Right next to it, you can find what changed, a graph tracking the changes, and all the things that affect your credit score. Those are the categories we have been talking about. They might not have the same name, but they serve the same purpose.

Once you know what is what, take a closer look at your credit score. Has it changed? Has it gone up, down? If it has, see what has impacted your score. They usually tell you, making it easy for you to find and understand. Inspect the category that has affected your score and make sure it is due to something you have done. You applied or opened a new card. You have a balance on one of your cards. Your average age of credit increased. Or a hard pull dropped from your history. When you see something that wasn't you, hit the dispute button and follow the process.

The second thing to do while monitoring your credit is evaluate every category one by one. You'd want to do this to compare your recent score to your past score. There should be no changes unless you used your score for a credit application. As usual, your categories are payment history and derogatory marks, utilization rate, age of credit, total accounts, and credit inquires.

Just so you have an idea, someone who has an almost perfect credit score of 800 has a credit score that looks something like this.

- Payment history: 100 percent

- Credit card use: 7 percent

- Derogatory marks: Zero

- Credit age: Twenty-five years
- Average age of credit: Seventeen years
- Total accounts: Twelve
- Hard inquiries: One [81]

In your case, your report will look something like this. Remember, you just started in the credit game.

- Payment history: 100 percent
- Credit card use: 0 percent
- Derogatory marks: Zero
- Credit age: Eleven months
- Average age of credit: Six months
- Total accounts: Three
- Hard inquiries: Three

After you go through every category of that report, there is one thing left to do: check all your other credit score apps. Really. You'd want to check every other app to compare credit scores and reports. The first few checks will take some time getting used to. Once you've done this over and over, it will just be a breeze.

Remember, each bank and app reports your scores in their own way. Each account you have has its own reporting period as well. Your credit scores will be somewhat different but very close to each other. The importance of checking your credit score frequently is not only to monitor your score but also monitor your report.

I'm not saying you should check your credit score every day like I did. Instead, you should monitor it occasionally.

---

81   Bev O'Shea, "What Is the Highest Credit Score? Can You Get a
      'Perfect' Score?" NerdWallet, December 16, 2020.

The importance of checking your score is to make sure there are no additional accounts on your name or a high utilization on a credit card.

Thankfully, whenever there is a hard inquiry on my credit, my phone blows up. Every app I use to track my credit, even the bank apps, send me a notification and an email to alert me of changes. This helps as a warning for whenever someone used my credit to open an account. They also provide me with the option to dispute whatever is on the report. This brings me some peace of mind.

To see how each category affects your credit score, visit me at LuccianoDiazSkoff.com and reach out on Instagram @LuccianoDiazSkoff.

CHAPTER 13.

Credit Toolbox

———

"An investment in knowledge pays the best interest."

—BENJAMIN FRANKLIN

As we know, time does not stop for anyone. Nor does life. Life is a series of events that mold our view of the world and others. Oftentimes we know why things happen, other times we don't. No matter what happens, we are always in control of how we react.

Our credit is subject to the same effects life has on us, with a slight difference. Most of the time, we can guess to a certain degree what will happen to our credit score. It is a very rational thing. For example, how buying a car or a house affects our credit, or how paying off a student loan is like closing an account. In this chapter, we'll discuss the factors that will make your credit fluctuate, as well as answer questions you haven't thought of.

***

You might find yourself in the process of shopping for a car or a home while reading this book. First, you should know that this process takes time. Time searching for the right car, time searching for the right dealer, and time searching for the best loan.

Your credit score will also take time coming back up after the hard inquiries from the banks show up on your report. The process of buying a car is not simple. You should know how it affects your credit score. Once you decide on a car and who to buy it from, choosing a lender is the next step.

Card dealers will send your application for a car loan to different banks. If each bank decides to open your application, an inquiry will show up on your report. Not only will you have the inquiries from the credit bureaus, but you will also have the inquiries of each bank whose offer you would like to see.

Some scoring models do not group the inquiries in your credit report, as well as some banks do not report the loan agreement after some time. Thankfully, in the new models, consumers can be sure there will only be one hard inquiry for their car loan as long as it is within a fifteen-day period. Some scoring models include inquiries in a thirty-day period. Hard inquires for mortgages are also grouped together.[82]

Auto loans can affect your score differently. It all depends on your payments. Once you buy a car, you will see an auto loan application on your credit report. The scoring models know that you are shopping for a car, so they will group

---

82 Jennifer White, "Multiple Inquiries When Shopping for a Car Loan," Experian, January 30, 2020.

every inquiry into one. This single inquiry will make your score drop because there is uncertainty on whether you can manage this new debt and because no other payment history is associated with this type of loan.

The only way to increase your score is by paying on time and not missing a payment. As we know by now, it will lower your score even further. Another thing to have in mind is once you get approved for your car loan, you will have a new score on your report. You already know the model for credit cards: either a FICO score or VantageScore. But with auto loans, you will see a separate score titled FICO auto score.[83] This is the score directly related to your car loans.

With homes, it is quite similar. The different credit bureaus use different FICO scoring models specifically designed to help banks decide whether to extend you the mortgage. When you apply for a mortgage, the lender uses either FICO scoring or VantageScore model to determine your creditworthiness. This process takes more time compared to buying a car.

You can prequalify for a mortgage from a bank, saving you from that hard inquiry. Most banks do that. Once you have chosen which bank will lend your mortgage, they will proceed to check your credit score. This first inquiry is the bank pulling your scores from the three major credit bureaus to understand where you are credit-wise. You will see your score drop, and it will not be your last.

The bank wants to know your lines of credit, your open accounts, your time handling credit, and how good

---

83   Sarah Brady, et. al., "What Is a FICO Auto Score and What Score Is Good?" Credit Karma, December 8, 2020.

are you at paying back. This process takes time, so do not get anxious. After a couple of weeks, or maybe even months, your score will come back up. And right around that time, the bank will hit your credit report with another hard inquiry, this time with a tool called Factual Data.

Factual Data is a leading provider of merged credit reports, flood zone determinations, and data verification services to the mortgage lending industry.[84] They also use this tool to see if you have undisclosed debt, trended credit data, and rescoring. It is a risk management tool for mortgage lenders.

After this hurdle, your score will drop again since it has a second hard inquiry in your report. This is why it is important not to add credit products to your report a minimum of six months prior to this process. Your credit score will take some hits.

Throughout the process, make sure you keep your credit utilization rate to a minimum, you do not apply for new lines of credit, and that there is no change in your income. Banks take all of this into account. But that's not all, because a third hard inquiry is waiting to happen.

The moment you accept your new mortgage, there will be a third hard pull on your credit score. And again, your credit score will drop. Not significantly, but it will. This process of buying a home typically takes around two months, give or take. Now, with the pandemic raging on and with executive orders going back and forth, we are looking at four to eight months.

---

84   "Resources," Factual Data, accessed December 31, 2020.

Two reasons banks take their time closing the deal are: 1) they need to know you can still pay the mortgage; and 2) there was no significant change in your credit score in that time (other than them checking your score).

A study found that the average credit score drop when purchasing a home is fifteen points. Some consumers have reported they've seen their credit slide by as much as forty points.[85]

You will hit your lowest score in this process an average of one hundred sixty days after your first inquiry.[86] And it will take another one hundred sixty days for your credit score to go back to normal. So, if you are in a hurry to increase your score after getting a mortgage, just know it will take almost a year. However, a car loan might lower your credit score by only two to seven points.[87]

As with both auto loans and mortgages, your credit score is a defining factor on your interest. To help you understand, ask yourself this question: "How much more will I pay with a not-so-good credit score?" The difference is an average of $45,000 in interest for a mortgage.[88] And for a car loan, it's close to $5,000.[89] So, think hard next time when buying a car or a home, and choose the right

85 Sarah O'Brien, "Buying a House Can Send Your Credit Score down. Here's How Long It Takes to Recover," CNBC, November 6, 2018.

86 Tendayi Kapfidze, "LendingTree Reveals How Buying a House Affects Credit Scores," LendingTree, October 31, 2018.

87 Gerri Detweiler, "How Much Will My Credit Score Drop If I Apply for a Car Loan?" Credit.com, April 16, 2018.

88 Jill Cornfield, "Your Credit Score Could Mean as Much as $45,000 in Savings... or Expenses," CNBC, July 23, 2018.

89 Liz Knueven, "Here's the Average Auto Loan Interest Rate by Credit Score, Loan Term, and Lender," *Business Insider*, December 8, 2020.

time. It is better to wait six months and increase your credit score than pay more than you should in interest.

Neither a car loan nor a mortgage will affect your credit utilization. On the contrary, they improve your credit mix, adding more credit products to your report.

***

It feels great to finally send the bank the last payment for the car loan, doesn't it? You should celebrate. The car is finally yours. You do not owe anyone anything regarding the car. At last, it is 100 percent yours!

But what happens to your credit score? Or your student loan? Or your mortgage? Bet you didn't think about that. But do not worry, it's nothing bad.

When you have paid a loan or a mortgage in full, the account status related to that changes to "paid." Often, when your credit history shows a significant change, your score dips. Although paying off a student or car loan is great news, you just closed an open account.

In other words, this means you just closed an account that you were paying on time and was in good standing. The change in your credit score is not the one you were expecting. Your score will certainly dip due to the reasons mentioned before.

Same as after buying a car or a home, your credit will bounce back up. In this case, your credit score will recuperate faster.

Remember, you were paying on time, every time, which helped your credit score stay high or increase. Now, since you closed an account, your credit score takes a hit. However, since you always paid on time, every time, and assuming you do not have any other negative mark in your credit history, your score will come back up in a few months. And since you closed the account in good standing, it will stay in your credit history for ten years as a positive account. This will certainly reflect positively on your credit score after a few months have passed.

***

You have fallen behind on your bills by thirty days, maybe sixty days, even ninety days, and you are worried a debt collector might contact you soon. Let me tell you, they will definitely contact you if you stopped paying an account. When will they call? It all depends on the statute of limitations of each state and territory. They will contact you as they see fit, not breaking the law, until you pay or accept a payment plan. There is always the option of not paying. And there are ways to stop collection agencies from contacting you.

There are different types of collection agencies as well as different types of collections. Let start with the latter. What is a collection? This is the action a debt holder takes in order to collect the debt. The debts that can be collected include credit card, medical, automobile loans, personal loans, business loans, student loans, and even unpaid utility and cellphone loans.

This collection mark appears on the account associated with your credit report, often affecting your credit score. Although, a collection mark that you will normally not see on your report is a mortgage debt or car loan. Unpaid mortgages generally end up in foreclosure and unpaid car loans usually lead to repossession.

In some states, lenders may still pursue you for the difference between what the repossessed car and foreclosure home received at auction and your loan balance. That amount can be sent to collections as well. Banks often send the account into collections after at least sixty days have passed from the original date of payment. This is when collectors come in.

There are two types of collectors or collection agencies. The debt collector, who works as a middleman, and a collection agency per se. When a bank understands that an account is delinquent or that there has not been a payment thirty, sixty, or 180 days after your first missed payment, they report the loan in your credit history as "charged off." This means the lender no longer expects to collect on it.[90]

The account that has been charged off will appear in your credit report as a transferred or closed account with no balance owed. This is a derogatory mark that will stay in your credit history for up to seven years. Thanks to the statute of limitations, charge-off and collection marks, by law, must be removed seven years after the original delinquency.

Once the account has been charged off, collectors come into play. A middleman of the bank, a hired debt collector, will contact you to get you to pay the debt. There are ways to stop them from contacting you or pay part of the debt and close the collection.

In this case, the bank does not want to make money, they simply want to settle the debt. When the debt is collected,

90   Jim Akin, "What Is a Charge-Off?" Experian, July 22, 2019.

the creditor typically pays the collectors 25 percent to 50 percent of the amount.[91] When a bank chooses to sell the debt to a collection agency, things change.

Collections are a business. Collection agencies are run as businesses, so they will want to make money from you. What collection agencies do after the account is delinquent is the following: Accounts in collection are often sold as a package or portfolio in a bidding process. Debt collectors purchase these packages in the process, usually paying 4 cents to the dollar of the face value. If the balance owed is $1,000, the debt collector bought it at $40.

Debt collectors also specialize in the type of debts. For example, a collection agency might collect only debts that owe less than $500 and are no older than two years. Also, the price of the debt depends on its age. The older the debt, the less it costs, thus making it less collectible.

The type of debt also influences the price. A mortgage is worth more than a utility bill. Debt collectors get paid when they collect. Since the collection agency buys the debt, when they collect, they do not send any of the amounts collected to the creditor.

Even old debts past the statute of limitations or otherwise deemed uncollectable are sold for pennies on the market, potentially making profits for collectors in that area.

If your account goes to collections, certain laws protect consumers. We all know or heard stories about collection agents calling insistently to collect or incurring unfair practices. Each state has its own statute of limitations.

In this case, the Federal Trade Commission (FTC) enforces the FDCPA, the main law prohibiting debt collectors from

---

91   Amy Fontinelle, "How the Debt Collection Agency Business Works," Investopedia, May 26, 2020.

using abusive, unfair, or deceptive practices to collect money. These practices include calling at all hours, pretending to be someone else, and harassment. The law also prohibits them from contacting others about your debt, requires them a written notice of procedure, and restricts unfair practices like depositing a post-dated check early.

This is a brief overview of how collectors should operate when collecting a debt: Collectors can use phone calls and letters to contact you and entice you to repay what you owe. They can do a thorough search of your accounts and assets and determine your ability to pay, which then they can pursue a court order to make this happen.

Even with a judgment for the debtor to pay, it can be difficult to collect the money. When this happens, collectors can place levies on bank accounts or motor vehicles to force you to pay. They can also try placing a lien on the property or forcing the sale of an asset. Collectors can even go to the extent of suing you to collect the debt.

One thing collectors will try to do is urge, persuade, or seduce you to pay some of the debt or agree to a payment program. This is a trick they use to extend the time limit of the debt. Since the moment you made a payment against the debt, no matter how much, the clock restarts. This means you could be months away from not having the collection mark in your report, but that single payment just restarted the seven-year count. Be aware of this tactic, as people could easily fall in this trap trying to show goodwill.[92]

---

92   Aaron Crowe, "How Do Debt Collection Agencies Work?: Everything You Need To Know," *Better Credit Blog | Credit Help For Bad Credit,* August 6, 2020.

Now, before being delinquent on your account, think about all the troubles you will go through with a collector and how it will affect your credit score. In the current model of scoring of FICO 8, unpaid and paid collections affect your score. In the new model, only the unpaid ones count. Nonetheless, the higher your credit score, the more points it will drop.

If you have excellent credit, you can expect a fifty-point drop in your credit score. If you are in the poor or very poor range of your credit, something like a ten-point drop can happen.[93]

Not only that, but back in the days (before 2008), if you had a collection come up in your credit report, lenders commonly participated in the abusive practice of "universal default." That means that a lender could raise your interest rate or charge you penalty fees or any additional fees if you went into default with another lender.

However, banks can still lower your credit limit or close your account if they believe you have lost your creditworthiness. Also, if you hold multiple accounts with the same lender you defaulted, the lender can change the terms and conditions of the other accounts you hold with them. Like I said earlier, a collection can stay on your credit report up to seven years. The seven-year count starts the moment you default on your debt, become delinquent on the account, or do not pay anything and the debt holder sends your account to collections.

At this point, you can do a couple of things. First thing is, if you have the resources to pay off the debt in full, you

---

93   Gideon Sandford, "How Do Collections Affect Your Credit? Top 10 Questions Answered," Credit Sesame, May 22, 2020.

can do so. This will close the collection the fastest. If you can't close the collection this way, you can negotiate a deal with the collection agency to repay, be it a monthly payment plan or pay a percentage of the payment. If the last approaches do not work for you or you simply do not want to pay, don't pay. Although, not paying means the collection will stay on your report until it drops, while paying could solve the issue faster.

Take, for example, my friend René. When he got his account sent to collection, he felt discouraged and neglected his credit for years. He tells me that every so often he receives phone calls from collection companies trying to collect the debt. "Every time they called, I said I did not have any money and told them to not call again. I used to get so many calls, I stopped answering." Little did he know that not answering calls and not agreeing to pay will help him in the long run. It also helped that he did not apply for any loan or credit card in the meantime.

But before you decide on any of the previous approaches to handling the debt, you should do something first. Make sure whoever is demanding payment, or collecting, has the legal right to do so.

Your account can be sold multiple times to different debt collectors and collection agencies. Each transaction must be properly documented. To verify that the collection agency owns your debt, you should send a debt validation letter to the agency. This should happen in the first thirty days of the agency contacting you. Until the debt is validated the agency cannot contact you nor collect the debt.[94]

---

94 "What Should I Do When a Debt Collector Contacts Me?" Consumer Financial Protection Bureau, accessed October 12, 2020.

An example letter to send the collection agency is:

[Your name]

[Your return address]

[Date]

Debt collector name]

Debt collector address]

Re: [Account number for the debt, if you have it]

Dear [debt collector name],

I am responding to your contact about collecting a debt. You contacted me by [phone/mail] on [date] and identified the debt as [any information they gave you about the debt].

I do not have any responsibility for the debt you're trying to collect. If you have good reason to believe that I am responsible for this debt, mail me the documents that make you believe that.

Stop all other communication with me and with this address, and record that I dispute having any obligation for this debt. If you stop your collection of this debt and forward or return it to another company, please indicate to them that it is disputed.

If you report it to a credit bureau (or have already done so), also report that the debt is disputed.

Thank you for your cooperation.

Sincerely, [your name]

Remember, do not agree to pay or acknowledge the debt in the letter. If the debt can't be validated, send all three credit bureaus a letter telling them to remove the collection, either by mail or email. You should follow up with them too.

This letter is provided by the Consumer Financial Protection Bureau (CFPB) and this is meant to be an example.[95] This is not legal advice. You can find more information on their website at ConsumerFinance.gov.

As long as you do not break the three rules we talked about (always have the cash before using your card, always pay in full, on time, and never having a balance) this should never happen to you. If it does, you have the tools and the knowledge to move forward and stay on track in your journey to financial freedom.

***

"Bankruptcies can damage your score and could prohibit you from taking on additional credit as creditors will be wary of lending to someone who has a history of nonpayment," Danielle Harrison, a certified financial planner in Columbia, Missouri, told CNBC Select in an interview.[96]

A bankruptcy is declaring to the law that you are unable to pay outstanding debts. Another definition is a person judged by a court to be insolvent whose property is taken and disposed of for the benefit of creditors.

---

95   "Sample Letters to Dispute Information on a Credit Report," Consumer Financial Protection Bureau, accessed October 12, 2020.

96   Elizabeth Gravier, "Filing for Bankruptcy Can Cause a Good Credit Score to Drop at Least 200 Points—Here's What You Should Know," CNBC, December 2, 2020.

I hope this never happens to anyone. We associate the word "bankruptcy" with failure, bad luck, sadness, stress, anxiety, and loneliness, all valid feelings and emotions that make our body ache. Alongside the feelings and emotions, your credit score also takes a toll.

Filing for bankruptcy causes your credit score to plummet more than two hundred points. Someone with a credit score of seven hundred eighty or above would be dinged between two hundred and two hundred forty points, while someone with a six hundred and eighty score would lose one hundred thirty to one hundred fifty points.[97]

But it can be used as a tool to help you. If this is your last resort, bankruptcy will help you pay off debt, liquidate assets, and get some type of financial relief. One constant that never changes is time. It is a foe while building your credit score but your best ally along the way. It is finite, but there is a lot of it.

Time will heal your credit score, it will solidify it for the future, and the more time you have with credit, the less the impact of opening new accounts. But time does not sit well with us when it comes to hard inquiries and collections. Nor does it with bankruptcy.

Like collections, a bankruptcy stays on your report for seven years. In this case, the amount of time with credit and lack of negative information in your report do little to minimize the impact of it. The presence of it and the time in your history are the factors for your credit score.

While a bankruptcy will lower your credit score dramatically, it does not mean that it cannot improve after the

---

97   Elizabeth Gravier, "Filing for Bankruptcy Can Cause a Good Credit Score to Drop at Least 200 Points—Here's What You Should Know," CNBC, December 2, 2020.

bankruptcy is gone. You can, and should, start working on your credit score right after the decision. You will see your credit score bounce back up in a couple of short years if you do things right.

The amount of debt in the bankruptcy will directly affect how big an impact it will have on your credit score. Bankruptcy, collections, and hard inquiries all affect your credit score in one way or another. The best thing you can do to remedy the effect is to let time take care of it and work on your credit.

As time passes, the impact on your credit lowers, thus helping you increase your credit score. And while you let time do its work, you should also start or keep working on your credit, not wait until the effects fall off your credit history.

Your credit is something you continuously work and improve upon. Remember, credit is a tool, and credit cards are the physical representation of it. Life happens and your credit will fluctuate, but as long as you keep working on it and taking care of it, it will always provide.

***

Ah, interests. The thing that no one cares about until it's time to pay. In almost every agreement involving money, the terms tell you how much, when to pay, what happens if you do not pay, and how much someone will charge you for using their money.

Now, if you always pay your balance in full and on time, you do not have to worry about interest. If you do not pay on time, which means you have a revolving balance, interest will show up in your debt. This interest is compounded daily, so on top of the late fees you need to pay, you also need to pay interest for every day you did not pay on time. (Thankfully, most banks have a grace period. You should check yours.)

This is the problem with credit card debt and a key point to consider when choosing a card: You'll never know when you will have to pay interest. But how do you know the exact amount you should pay if you have an APR of 15 percent?

We've talked about APR before; this is the annual percentage rate of your card. To calculate the amount of interest you will pay for every day you are late, divide the APR by the total of days in a year, or APR divided by 365 days. And since APR is a percentage, it is percent per day. With a 15 percent APR, and 365 days in a year, the math is as follows: 15 percent / 365 = 0.041 percent per day.[98]

So, if your card has a 15 percent APR, you will be paying 0.041 percent of interest for every day you did not pay on time. Since interests are accrued daily over your daily balance, and you keep using the card that you still have not paid off, the additional amount comes into play when calculating interest. This means that the amount you owe will be greater than the original debt.

That is not all: Not everyone has the same APR. The APR is determined the moment you get approved using your credit score and disposable income. When you review a card's information, you will likely see an APR section

98   "How to Calculate Credit Card APR Charges," Chase, accessed December 31, 2020.

with a range of percent. For example, a card has a variable APR of 15.99 percent to 27.98 percent. For strong applicants with an excellent credit score, they can expect to have the lowest APR on the spectrum. For those not so good applicants, they should expect otherwise.

When interest starts creeping up on your account, you should stop and analyze your spending habits to mitigate, lower, and stop paying interest. Here are a couple of things you can do to avoid paying interest. Use a 0 percent APR credit card. This is the best way of not paying any interest for some time. Another way to avoid paying interest, which you should know by now, is paying on time and in full. This works 100 percent of the time. Stop using that card until you pay it off. Like I said, interest accrues daily on the daily balance you have.

Interest is the cost of borrowing money. They also provide certain compensation for the risk of borrowing money. In some instances, your interest can fluctuate. Most of the time, your interest rate changes based on the market's supply and demand.

Interest rates are a factor of the supply and demand of credit: An increase in the demand for money or credit will raise interest rates, while a decrease in the demand for credit will decrease them. Conversely, an increase in the supply of credit will reduce interest rates, while a decrease in the supply of credit will decrease them.[99]

You actually have something to do with the supply and demand of credit in the market. Let's say you go to a bank and open a bank account, and you deposit money in the

---

99   Reem Heakal, "What Are the Forces Behind Interest Rates and What Causes Them to Rise?" Investopedia, August 5, 2019.

account. The bank then uses that money to lend it to other people. That is one of the things they do with your money. The more banks can lend, the more credit available in the economy, thus decreasing the price of borrowing, or interest rates, due to the increase of credit supply.

Now, what happens if instead of opening an account, you decide not to pay this month's debt until next month. You decrease the amount of credit available in the market. You see, this then triggers a small rise in the economy's interest rates. This decision will not only increase the interest rate in the economy, but you also increase the amount of interest you have to pay on your debt.

Another factor that increases interest rates, and also tied to the economy, is inflation. Lenders will start to demand higher interest values as compensation for the decrease of purchasing power of the money they are paid in the future. These interest rates increase and decrease every so often, all across the board. This goes for mortgages, car loans, student loans, credit cards, and so on.

The most helpful tool you have to access the lowest interest rates, even when the economy is not doing so great, is your credit score and your credit history. This is another reason why building your credit score early, and building it right, will serve you in the future.

You might find yourself buying a property or an asset when the rest of the world thinks it is not the right time to buy. Your credit, and time, will be determining factors on when to buy and how much you will pay. The main factor for us credit card users is our own credit score. This will determine how much interest rate we will have to pay if we have a balance on our account.

Our credit score will also help lenders determine how much risk of not paying we can be when borrowing money, thus determining how much money we can borrow. As long as you keep your credit score above seven hundred forty and you continue to use your credit, you will be able to access the best interest rates in the market along higher credit limits. Remember, if you do not want to worry about paying interest rates, always pay in full and on time.

***

Can I have multiple cards of the same card? The answer is yes, but it depends when, how, and who is the issuer. You can absolutely have two identical cards on separate accounts. You would normally do this when the card you are using has a cap on rewards or points. This cap limits you on how many points you can earn, so the idea of having a second identical card is to keep reaping the benefits of the card.

Let's say card A has a set limit of points you can earn. Typically, what banks do is tell you that you can earn four times the points in the first $5,000 spent on a category, then it is 1 percent. They usually do this per year. On the other hand, you know you exceed your spending in that category and you do not want to miss the points. You take out the same card, and when you max out the points in one card, you switch to the other one to keep maximizing your points. It is that simple.

Once you max out the rewards, combine them to do whatever you want. But there is a caveat, and it depends on time and the issuer. Issuers have caught up to the credit card churners and to the people who only use the cards for the points. If you have an Amex Gold and have already earned the welcome bonus, even if you get approved for the same card, you will not earn the welcome bonus of the card even if it is a different one. Another issuer tackling this issue is Chase and Citi. They will not let you earn a sign-up bonus if you received one for the same card in the past twenty-four months.

Credit card issuers are also wary of accepting identical accounts because of the associated risk. They believe that by having two identical accounts, or cards, you are more prone to run them up and not pay. As always, there is a way around this. First, if you are looking to earn the same reward bonus repeatedly, time your credit card applications. This will help you in your process of getting the sign-up bonuses. To do that, you need to read the fine print, which is our second point. Read the small letters and make sure you know how this will affect you in the future.

If you want an identical card but the issuer does not allow you to, do the following: Apply for the same credit card, but with a business account. American Express currently has three different platinum cards: the personal Amex Platinum, the business Amex Platinum, and the Charles Schwab Amex Platinum. You can only get this last product if you have a Charles Schwab brokerage account. For the other two, you can apply for either even if you have one or the other.

Since a personal credit card and a business credit card are a different product, even if identical, you will have two of the same cards. Sometimes the issuer might even approve you for a second identical card. If you do not have a business, take the next approach. Get approved for a different product version of the card, and after a couple of months select to upgrade or downgrade. This approach will let you earn the sign-up bonus of the other card by doing a product change for the card you want.

To learn how to calculate the interest you will be paying in your balance or learn how to prepare your credit report for purchasing a car or a home, visit me at LuccianoDiazSkoff.com and reach out on Instagram @LuccianoDiazSkoff. You can find all sorts of tools and resources like these, including scripts, dispute letters, and guides on how to rebuild your credit after a bankruptcy.

CHAPTER 14:

Where Is My Identity?

———

"Social security, bank account, and credit card
numbers aren't just data. In the wrong hands,
they can wipe out someone's life savings, wreck
their credit, and cause financial ruin."

—MELISSA BEAN

As Sweden inches forward to being completely cash-less (only 13 percent of Swedes reported used cash for a recent purchase), we still have some way to go.[100] In contrast, roughly less than 60 percent of people in the United States have a credit card.[101] That is 40 percent of people who are missing out on a great opportunity. Why should everyone have a credit card? Because it has become a modern tool to achieve your financial freedom.

---

100 Maddy Savage, "Sweden's Cashless Experiment: Is It Too Much Too Fast?" NPR, February 11, 2019.

101 Jamie Gonzalez-Garcia and Allie Johnson, "Credit Card Ownership Statistics," CreditCards.com, January 15, 2020

We live in a modern world where almost everything is digital. While we buy things on Amazon, our credit card becomes more of a key rather than a card. That key, though, has some information that, if not protected, could damage your credit score, history, and even your identity.

Thankfully, cards know this, and they have systems and protocols in place to protect you from these everyday threats. Most of the credit card issuers now have a twenty-four seven customer service department available if something happens to your card.

For example, someone, somewhere, managed to get all my card's information and used it to buy things off the internet. My bank caught the transactions on time, sadly not before they went through, and managed to cancel my card before anything else was bought. I had to file a report with the bank, which a representative helped me out with, and the money they spent was credited to my account within thirty days.

"My credit card company calls me if it looks like I've bought too many hoodies and cargo pants for my kid at Old Navy."[102]
—CHRISTY LEMIRE

That is the type of service I want with all my cards. A study by J.D. Power ranks credit cards by customer satisfaction. For all of you looking for a new card, this can help you make a decision. American Express ranked the highest, followed by Discover and Bank of America third for the year 2020.[103] If you hold any of these cards, I can say you are in good hands.

---

102 Christy Lemire Lemire, "Review: 'Identity Thief' Has No Charge," telegram.com, February 9, 2013.

103 "2020 U.S. Credit Card Satisfaction Study," J.D. Power, August 20, 2020.

So what happens if your credit card gets lost or stolen? Do not worry, banks are ready for this. As soon as you notice your card is missing, call the card issuer and report it missing or stolen. If, in fact, it is only missing and you find it, you can ask for the bank to unlock the card to keep using it. Otherwise, if the card is lost, they will close the account and send you a new card with a new number.

If your card is used while it is stolen and you filed the report, you will not be liable for anything bought with your card. This is the importance of acting fast. When you do call the card issuer to report a card stolen, they will need to verify your identity. You will likely need to share information with them, such as your name, physical address, social security number, and maybe a keyword or your PIN.

Once you have provided that information, they will need to verify your last transactions made with the card. You should have your bank statement at hand when the call happens to speed up the process. You can download it from your bank's page.

After you finish the process, you will receive your new card without any effect on your credit score or report. Remember to always check your credit card statement to be aware of your credit card usage and look for payments or transactions you did not do or authorize.

Let's say that one day, while checking your statement, you see an unusual number of transactions on your card. In your head, you go over the times you used your card in the last month. Then, you remember one instance where you used your card, but there was a problem with the machine. You saw your card being swiped a couple of times before they handed it back. Did you have a fishy feeling?

Most probably, while you were distracted with skipping the song on your phone, they skimmed your card. Someone swiped your card on another device that captured your credit card's information. A couple of hours later, your information was already being used to buy things off the internet or being sold to identity thieves.

This is one of the modalities used to capture your personal information. Your identity can be used to take out credit cards in your name. Your information could also be used for someone else's identity or could even be sold to whoever wants to harm you or take your money.

Another way identity theft happens is by not disposing of your trash correctly, leaving behind documents with sensitive information. They can also get your information by stealing your mail. They may also call you or send emails on behalf of someone else and you share personal information. This is most commonly known as phishing.

Additional identity theft modalities include straightforward theft, stealing documents, pickpocketing, conning someone into sharing your information and, on those same lines, address manipulation. As Peter Keane, dean emeritus and professor at the Golden Gate University College of Law, says, "The human imagination and creativity are endless when it comes to stealing things."[104]

In the very serious and very possible scenario where your identity is stolen, here are the steps you should take

104 Odysseas Papadimitriou, "Identity Theft: What It Is, How It Happens & the Best Protection," WalletHub, December 8, 2020.

to minimize the damage. To gather that your identity has been stolen, the FTC (Federal Trade Commission) provides the following clues:

- You see withdrawals from your bank account that you can't explain.
- You don't get your bills or other mail.
- Merchants refuse your checks.
- Debt collectors call you about debts that aren't yours.
- You find unfamiliar accounts or charges on your credit report.
- Medical providers bill you for services you didn't use.
- Your health plan rejects your legitimate medical claim because the records show you've reached your benefits limit.
- A health plan won't cover you because your medical records show a condition you don't have.
- The IRS notifies you that more than one tax return was filed in your name or that you have income from an employer you don't work for.
- You get a notice that your information was compromised by a data breach at a company where you do business or have an account.[105]

You should take immediate action to mitigate the risk of further damage. Usually, the person who stole your identity had the intention or is in the market of stealing and selling identities or it has been bought to drain you of your money.

---

105 "Warning Signs of Identity Theft," Consumer Information, February 19, 2019.

They can take credit cards in your name, open accounts, or get medical treatment on your insurance. Once you noticed these things, there are ten steps to take right after your identity is stolen.

1. File a report with the Federal Trade Commission. They will build a file with your identity theft information and use it on hand with other departments to further protect you.

2. Contact your local police department and file an identity theft report with them. Although they won't be able to prosecute anyone online or overseas, this information helps them track people who steal identities in your community and be aware of anyone who might be using it.

3. Notify the IRS and your identity theft insurance, if applicable. If you find out your identity was used to file an income tax return, then someone else got your refund.

4. Place a fraud alert on your credit reports. It is free, and it further protects your credit from anyone trying to misuse it. This request alerts the three major credit bureaus—Equifax, Experian, and TransUnion—that your identity might have been compromised. Since it stays on your report for a year, anyone trying to get a card in your name will raise an alert and notify the bureaus. This way they take an extra security step to verify the identity of the person.

5. Freeze your credit. This action will completely cut off access to your credit report. The credit bureaus will not share your report with anyone who requests it. You can freeze and unfreeze your credit directly with the bureaus. This action is also free.

6. Sign up for a credit monitoring service, if offered. Credit card issuers might offer you a credit monitoring service to protect you. You should consider getting it if you believe this can happen again or are still worried your information is around.

7. Tighten security on your accounts. Although it may seem obvious, most people never change their passwords. Start going through every webpage you have an account, like your email, streaming services, and others, and change the password. Even your browser could help you with this one. There are also apps designed to come up with passwords and store them for you.

8. Nowadays, almost every webpage that needs your email and password to access it has a two-step verification. This means that on top of entering your password, you receive a code through a call, text message, or email, or answer a very personal question. This helps tighten your security on the internet.

9. Review your credit reports for mystery accounts. Ask the three credit bureaus to send you a free credit report and look for suspicious accounts. Later, I will tell you how to fight those and other things in your report.

10. Scan credit card and bank statements for unauthorized charges.

11. Open new credit card and financial accounts. Even though you may have accounts that might not have been compromised, it is advised to open new accounts for further protection.[106]

---

106 Maryalene LaPonsie, "10 Things to Do If Your Identity Is Stolen," *U.S. News & World Report*, August 12, 2020.

This kind of fraudulent activity might go unnoticed for several reasons: you do not check your credit report, nor your bank statement, or simply you have not used a card in a while. Yes, the last time you used a card and stored it away might have been the moment your card information was taken.

In 2019, 14.4 million consumers became victims of identity fraud—about one in fifteen people.[107] Think of your friends, family members, and colleagues. One of them has been or will be a victim of identity fraud.

That's not all. There's a new victim of identity theft every two seconds. And in 2019 alone, consumers lost more than $1.9 billion to identity theft and fraud. The worst statistic of all is that one in five victims of identity theft have experienced it more than once. I do not mean to scare you with identity theft. I just want to make sure you know this happens and that you have the tools to protect yourself if this happens to you. It is important to protect ourselves when we are on the internet and when sharing our personal information.

Someone close to my family went through this. She asked me not to use her name, so let's call her Josefina. One day, she woke up to the amazing smell of Puerto Rican coffee her husband had prepared. As per her usual morning routine, she meditated, watched the news, and checked her email. While checking her email, she notices a couple of notifications at 3:00 a.m. from Credit Karma and myFICO. She told me, "At first, I thought it was the apps telling

---

107 "Facts + Statistics: Identity Theft and Cybercrime," Insurance Information Institute, accessed July 21, 2020.

me they updated my report. Then I read, 'There's a new inquiry on your report.' And that's when I freaked out."

Josefina then tried logging in to her accounts, but she couldn't. They not only applied for more than eight credit cards, but they had also hacked and changed her username and password on her accounts. In the coming days, as she talked with the credit bureaus and the banks, denied letters kept coming in. "That was the second scariest thing of all, after not knowing who had hacked me and what information they had, was the number of letters that I got from all the banks after their application was denied."

After long days of talking with each of the banks and each of the credit bureaus, Josefina regained access to her accounts. She put a freeze on her credit, got a password manager to change the accounts, and bought an identity protection plan. Occasionally, she still gets emails and phone calls from people trying to scam her. "I think my information is still out there. But thank God that was the only time that has happened."

Josefina recalls that all the denied letters said the same thing: too many inquires in a limited period. "I think that is what saved me," she told me. After she explained everything to the bureaus and the banks had everything in order, she was able to dispute and eliminate all the hard inquiries on her report.

To start protecting your identity from possible theft, you can do a couple of things right now. First, freeze your credit. This is a free service that you can get directly from your bank and from the credit bureaus. Anyone who wants to look at your credit won't be able to. Remember, you must lift your freeze if you are applying for a card, loan, or mortgage.

For those of you who buy most of your things on the internet, you can do a few things to protect your information too. First, turn on your firewall. It is your own computer's defense system against unauthorized access. When logging into accounts, make sure you do not repeat passwords. A great tool for this is a password generator and manager. Instead of thinking about it, you can automatically generate a password for your account, and the password manager will save it for next time. Most password generators offer you a VPN. This is the third thing you should get. A virtual private network (VPN) gives you online privacy and anonymity. This protects your computer's ID on the web.

The fourth thing for you to do is enable two-factor authentication. When logging into an account, you not only need the password, but you will also need a code. This further protects your logins and accounts from anyone who already has your email and password. You can set up your two-factor authentication through your phone. Use an authenticator app for this. Instead of receiving the code through text, you must have your phone and app open to enter the code. Connecting the app with the password manager is the best way. The app will autogenerate codes every thirty seconds, thus increasing the level of security.

On top of two-factor authenticators, you can use a security key. That is a physical USB key you have to insert into your computer and physically push a button to log in. If you do not have that key, there is no way of logging in. That is the fifth thing you can do.

Lastly, sign up for identity theft protection. This will help you monitor your identity and protect yourself. You can also get reimbursed for any money you lost as a consequence of the theft.

As long as you protect your information and don't share it with an unknown person or source, your chances of being targeted are slim—but still possible. If you fall victim to identity theft, you know what to look for and how to proceed.

To learn more about tools and measures you can use to protect yourself from identity theft, visit me at LuccianoDiazSkoff.com and reach out on Instagram @ LuccianoDiazSkoff.

PS—Our coffee here in Puerto Rico is so good, it is coined the coffee of "popes and kings", and the gift of choice in the Vatican.[108][109] The current and past popes preferred it. [110]

108 "Specialty Coffee Brands to Taste in Puerto Rico," Discover Puerto Rico, accessed September 5, 2020.

109 "Puerto Rico Coffee Roasters Alto Grande," Puerto Rico Coffee Roasters, accessed August 21, 2020.

110 "Puerto Rico Coffee History," A Cup Of Puerto Rico, November 15, 2017.

CHAPTER 15.

Top of the Mountain

———

"In childhood, a library card takes you to exotic, faraway places; in adulthood, a credit card does."

—EVAN ESAR

By this point, if you followed the credit card game plan, you should be ready to apply for your fourth card. There you go! I see you making the moves! A new world of opportunity is open for you. Offers will soon start coming in the mail about "how this card is right for you."

You can now shop around in the big leagues for cards that earn four times the points on this, three times the points on that, and another three times the points on other things. And the possibilities are endless. You are around the twelve-month credit building mark, or you waited a little bit longer. That is fine too. You have been carefully tracking and building your credit for a year now. And the only way to celebrate is by getting approved for your fourth card. Now you can choose a really good card that not only caters to your everyday needs, but it will also give you benefits and points your other cards could not really compete with.

Ideally, this new credit card will cover the gaps the other cards don't and will most likely add benefits like credit for food delivery or lounge access. And you can now choose between cards that either give you cash back or points, or one that fits a long-term goal like paying with points for a flight. Personally, I choose the card that is better for me at that point. Choosing between points and cash back is more a preference than an advantage. You could argue that points are worth more here rather than there. And some might say they'd rather have the cash in hand instead of points. It is up to you and what you like.

For me, the card I went with as my fourth card was the American Express Gold, an exceptional card all around. Now accepted in 99.9 percent of establishments around the country, the perks are unbelievable. I'll be sticking with this card for a while. When I got approved for this card, I had a seven hundred fifty-one VantageScore 3.0 based on TransUnion data. I also used the prequalified link Amex provides to make sure I fit their requirements for the card. The prequalified page also offered me a better welcome bonus than the promotion had. Instead of the usual thirty-five thousand points, I got the sixty thousand point offer. There was even one with a seventy-five thousand point welcome bonus. Sadly, that was not offered in Puerto Rico.

Once the card got home, I shared with my family what I had just done. I got myself my first American Express Gold card. Personally, I really wanted to do this to show myself I could. And to show you that it is not hard. You just have to know how. With my fifth card, I have locked in my everyday cards. These are the cards I always have in my wallet. This is because they all have a specific use.

I have my Amex Gold card for when I go dining, because they give me four times the points on restaurants, take-out, and delivery. I use my Chase Freedom Unlimited (CFU) whenever I go to the supermarket. Even though Amex also gives me four times the points on supermar-kets, CFU has a 5 percent cash back on groceries for the first year. This card also has a 3 percent cash back on drugstore purchases. For gas, Discover has me covered with the two times cash back on gas stations. With Dis-cover, I still have six months to go to earn as much cash back as I can in the first year, where Discover matches everything back. So by next year, if I have $300 in cash back, Discover will give me another $300 for cash back. They all have their functions and specialties.

Lastly, my fourth card is the Premia card from Banco Popular. This card is more like an honorable mention that has saved me a couple of times from a *papelón* (Puerto Rican slang word for embarrassment). This Premia card comes in handy when I do not have cash in my pockets, which I never do, and when the place I'm in doesn't pro-cess any of my other three cards. That is why you always need a card in your wallet that is accepted everywhere.

Well, that is the rundown of the cards I am currently car-rying in my wallet. One card for dining, one card for gas, another card for groceries, and one for when the others aren't accepted. Another thing you could do is switch out your back up card for an everyday card. For example, I could swap out my Premia card for another card that has

2 percent on other purchases. In my case, I did not do that since my CFU has the perk of 1.5 percent cash back on all other purchases. Of course, your everyday carry cards can change, and they should. They should be tempered to your lifestyle or current situation. You can bet once the pandemic is over, one or more cards will be swapped out for better cards that suit me.

Recent changes in the credit card landscape have made it possible for newcomers to start in the credit game. These new cards have made building credit and earning points accessible to everyone. They work and operate like a credit card, with a slight difference.

We got used to applying for a credit card where the issuer would check our credit score. Now, that is not the case. Instead of doing a hard pull on your credit, they base their decision on your income or what you have in your bank account. Some cards lean more on your monthly income, others on the savings you have. It all depends on what you want. Either way, it is an amazing tool to start building your credit.

Some examples of the previously mentioned cards are:

- Tomo card: https://TomoCredit.com
- X1 card: https://X1CreditCard.com
- Petal: www.PetalCard.com
- One: www.OneFinance.com
- Jasper: www.JasperCard.com
- Grain: https://TryGrain.com

They all have their own unique system of credit. That means that each has its own APR, credit model, financial structure, and niche customers. With that said, I do not know any of the companies, nor do I know if they will still be operational for years to come. This is just an example of credit card products that are revolutionizing how we build credit.

What comes after a year or so of building credit, having three or four cards under your belt, and maybe a personal loan? Not much. At least for a year. You have already built and grown your credit score from three hundred or so to around seven hundred twenty or seven hundred forty. You have a couple of hard inquiries on your credit. Your oldest one still has a year to drop from your report and another that is four months old. At this time, let your credit grow and mature. Let it breathe. Do not hit it with another hard inquiry or hard pull. Let it sit for a while. Keep paying your bills in full and on time. Keep your utilization rate under 9 percent or 0 percent, which is even better. And do not carry a balance.

Now that you have your fourth card on hand, you can do one of two things: keep those four cards forever and miss out on the points and miles. Or, what you all came here for, keep building your credit and playing the game. As we enter a new chapter in the points and miles game, I want to let you know a couple of things. Take this as a recommendation from a friend.

THINGS YOU NEED TO KNOW TO KEEP PLAYING THE GAME

Really, there is no wrong way to play it. As long as you hit your goals and use the cards for your benefit, that is the only thing that matters. As you continue to build your credit, your application strategy becomes really important. Rules like Chase's five twenty-four rule make their credit cards the first to get. You might blow your chance of getting a Chase card by following other cards with no rules. And if we are being honest, American Express is probably one of the easiest cards to get approval.

Get cards from banks that have a strict application rule. Maximize those points and get more out of those cards. On the topic of points: they aren't equal. American Express MR points aren't equal to Chase UR points. When staying in a hotel, one night can be cheaper than the other if you pay with these points instead of the other. That does not mean that they are worthless, it just means they are different currency.

Since each is its own currency, each has its own value, not only overall, but also when converting them for miles and nights. The value of your points will be determined if you fly coach, business, or first class. The same thing applies when booking a night at a hotel. Your point values are not necessarily the same as someone else's points.

The best approach for points is to have flexibility. Instead of putting all your points in one basket, you can transfer points back and forth in any category. This might be the best way of earning them, instead of just earning miles for one single airline.

As we have mentioned, not all points have the same value or access to the same redemption option. This is where diversifying your points come in handy. Redeeming points for hotels in Chase might provide you a better points value than American Express points. Amex, on the other hand, has better airline partners, delivering better bang for your points.

It will take you time to know which programs have the highest conversion rate for points. That is why it is important to be flexible. To continuously benefit from using your points, you must be able to move your points or use one program instead of the other. If you are too rigid when redeeming, you might lose an offer or the chance to get more value out of your points. And that can be discouraging for you.

Although you can use your points to travel for free, I hate to break it to you, it is rarely ever free. Traveling for free doesn't happen very often. You can use those points to book the flight, but you still have to pay taxes and fees. That welcome bonus does come in handy, but you still need to pay for food or Wi-Fi on the flight.

A very important thing to do with your points is to redeem them. This might sound crazy, but some people get redemption paralysis. In other words, they are just afraid they aren't redeeming the points for the right value, or they just don't want to use their points. My best advice in this case is to use the points. It is better to use them and travel rather than to not use them and lose their value.

When in the process of redeeming and using points, you should always do the math. You might see a couple of You-Tube videos that tell you how that person used the points. That is not necessarily true for you. You have a different lifestyle and different needs than the other person. To make sure you are using your card the right way, compare your card to other cards in the same redemption category. That way, you can do the math on how much benefit and value that card is giving you.

Lastly, keep learning. This takes time and practice to learn. Choose one or two programs and get comfortable with them. Once you know how the program works, jump to the next one. You'll find some programs have niche uses while others do not compare to the best. Each program has its own learning curve. You can choose to learn the basics or become an expert on it. Either way, it takes time.

If you do not understand something, ask. There is a whole community of experienced and new cardholders eager to share their knowledge. The points, miles, and cash back game is one we can all win. By having a strategy, timing your applications, and understanding the rules of the game, you can travel the world for a fraction of the price. Who wouldn't want that?

My last piece of advice: Enjoy the perks and benefits your cards have. Track what is left to hit that welcome bonus. Plan what you will do with the points and cash back. Give yourself time to appreciate where you are and relish how you built your credit. Most importantly, share this knowledge with family members, friends, colleagues, partners, professors, and people everywhere. Give them the tools you now have so they can start building their own credit and forging the base for their own financial freedom. Financial literacy is the only tool we have to break generational chains.

Let us all have freedom in credit cards.

Takeaways

———

*"A good financial plan is a road map
that shows us exactly how the choices we
make today will affect our future."*

—ALEXA VON TOBEL

I tracked and wrote down every detail of my credit score since the day I started building credit. The goal, for me, was to share it with you. My intention was to show that you don't need to be scared of credit cards. They are an advantage, not an anchor.

We have learned how banks and financial institutions determine our credit score. Our creditworthiness is determined by five factors: payment history and derogatory marks (35 percent), utilization rate (30 percent), age of credit (15 percent), total accounts (10 percent), and credit inquires (10 percent). These five categories are 100 percent of your credit score.

With that model, they give us a credit score between three hundred and eight hundred fifty. The higher your credit score, the better. To keep your score in top shape, you have to always pay in full, on time, and never carry a balance. If you need to have a balance, keep it under 10 percent of your total credit limit.

Your first two cards will build your credit backbone. They will be your longest credit lines, thus aging your credit as time goes by. Do not close them at any cost. The longer your credit cards are open, the better your credit score tends to be. Banks and financial institutions like to see that you are responsible with your cards. This includes keeping long accounts open and having a variety of credit products, from a couple of cards to a car loan and a mortgage.

Income is the determining factor banks use to determine your credit limit. The higher your income, the higher your limit, and vice versa. This is part of their risk assessment to determine if you will be able to pay your debt on time. If they see that you do, they will gladly increase your credit limit.

Throughout the book, we discussed timing and making decisions. This is what your first cards taught you: when to apply, how to apply, and which is the best card for you and your lifestyle. As with every game, this game has its rules too. Learn them, practice them, and beat the game. There is no trick. The rules are written down and are the same for everyone.

Most people get scared thinking that is how they lose by following the rules. We learned that playing by the rules is how we win. The key here is to not let yourself go with all the benefits that later end up hurting you. You will have the right mindset to not change your lifestyle for the card and still make the most out of it.

So, let's plan ahead. There are two approaches you can take when building your credit: the Freedom in Credit Cards approach and a conservative approach. Let's start with the first approach. Freedom in Credit Cards will get you twice the cards in the same amount of time while still getting cards with excellent perks.

In plan A, in month zero, go to the branch of a local bank and ask to apply for a credit card. When approved, try to start with two credit cards instead of one. This will be the starting base for building your credit. Monitor your credit for the coming months. Around month seven to nine, and with a credit score of over seven hundred twenty, apply for your third card. This will depend on what happened at month zero.

Congrats on your new card! Now, with your third card, let your credit recuperate for a couple of months. Keep monitoring your credit for the next round. Around month ten to twelve, with your credit score over seven hundred forty, shoot for your fourth card. Excellent! In twelve months you have four cards, two with awesome perks, and a credit score of over seven hundred forty!

If you got approved for only one card at month zero, let's go for plan B. As always, monitor your credit for the following months. In month six, you should go for your second card. Your credit score will most probably be around seven hundred ten. That's not bad as long as you are above seven hundred. With your second card on hand, start planning for your third card. In month nine, you are in the sweet spot to apply for the next card. You have a whole month to think about and choose the day to apply. Your credit score will probably be higher than the last time you applied. Go get it!

At last, you are on track to your fourth card in twelve months. When, in the month you got your third card will determine when you will apply for your fourth card. If you applied early or in the middle of the month, you can apply in the last week of month twelve. Now, let's say you applied on the twenty-eighth of month nine. Your bank will use that date as the end-cycle date for your account, thus updating your information to the credit bureaus in around five working days. In other words, you will have your credit score updated with new information the next month, moving your schedule to apply from month twelve to month thirteen. That is alright, since the bank you are applying to for your fourth card will see new information. Use that to your advantage.

Congrats on getting four credit cards in twelve months! In both plan A and plan B of getting credit cards the Freedom in Credit Cards way, you have a solid credit profile. By the time you apply for your third and fourth cards, two cards have already built up your credit, thus helping you apply for better cards with better perks and benefits.

Now, if for some reason those plans are not for you, take the Freedom in Credit Cards conservative route. From anywhere in the world, you can get on a computer and apply for a secured credit card. This will be your first card. For the next six months, you will use this card, take care of the card, and monitor your credit. In month six, get another secured credit card. And you are set. There is nothing more to do. You have two credit cards in your profile, and in six months more your oldest card will be one year old. You've done it!

The sole purpose of the conservative route is to start building credit. This route is perfect if that is what you want. Now, if you want to take advantage of the benefits and perks credit cards can offer as soon as possible, plan A is for you. In both cases, after one year of building credit, you can start applying for cards every three months or so.

I get asked frequently about the sign-up bonus and the process of applying for a card. When you earn the welcome bonus, you still get the points or the cash back you have accrued while earning the bonus. Let's say you needed to spend $500 in three months to get the $200 cash-back bonus. When you do, you will see that the $500 earned you $7 of cash back. When that bonus comes in, you will have $207 in your account.

Although authorized users are not taken into count in the most recent FICO update, the youngest person you can make an authorized user varies from bank to bank. Some vary between the ages of eight and thirteen. Others have no minimum age limit as long as they have a social security number.

If you are from a foreign country and you want to start building credit in Puerto Rico, USA, or any of its territories, you need to get yourself a social security number (SSN). If you are not eligible for an SSN, you may apply for an individual taxpayer identification number (ITIN) by the IRS. Visit a social security office for help and guidance.

If you are repeatedly denied for credit cards because of your physical address, check your credit report at AnnualCreditReport.com and make sure your address is correct. If it isn't, go to your local USPS postal office and ask to update your address. You can also go directly to the bank and the credit bureau that has your incorrect address and change it. Once that is done, make sure it is correct across all the bureaus and important offices.

The moment you get declined for a different reason, do not wait the five to seven days to get an answer. Do not waste your time and call the reconsideration line. Every bank has one. Ask to talk with a bank representative. Remember, an algorithm declined you, not the person over the phone. You might have been declined for lack of credit, too much credit line recently, or a bank rule. You should weigh your odds before applying. When unsure, look in online forums and groups and search for recent data points to make your decision.

But back to speaking with the bank representative: He is a human being, as we all are. Treat the person with respect. Explain your situation: why you want the card, how you will use it, and how it will be a great tool for you. Tell them you trust the bank, you believe in what they do, and you wouldn't have chosen any other bank. Most of the time, you will get your application approved as long as you are diligent and respectful. Embrace the awkward silence, and don't take no as a final answer.

Ask what they can do for you. If you are still not accepted for the card, do not despair. Search for the hard inquiry and dispute it with the credit bureaus. Most, if not all, credit apps come with the service of disputing an inquiry right in the platform. Use it for your benefit.

Ask for a product change when you do not take full advantage of a card, either because you do not use the perks or the annual fee outweighs the benefits. Instead of closing the card, tell the bank to change the card for another that you know you will benefit from.

When starting in the credit game, remember the three cardinal rules: 1) Do not use your card if you do not have the money cash (there are exceptions); 2) never carry a balance; and 3) always pay in full and on time. These three actions will build trust with your banks. This same trust will help you get higher credit limits and loans.

By following these three simple rules, you will never need to worry about interest, APRs, minimum payments, late fees, or anything else. The key for this whole game is time. That is an unwritten rule most people do not talk about.

Have you ever played monopoly? What do most people do when they go to jail? They use the card or pay to get out. The actual benefit of jail is that you do not risk paying rent for three turns when the table is full of properties. What does this have to do with credit cards? Time, and timing. Your best allies.

Conclusion: Freedom in Credit Cards

The end of this book is the start of your financial journey. With luck, I've been able to share with you all the information, resources, and tools to play and win at the credit card game. At his point, and with all you know, all you can do is grow. Once you understand the game and play it, you can succeed. Now, with four credit cards in your pocket, a year of experience, and this book, you can do as you like with credit cards. You got the hang of it. With this education and knowledge, you can leverage your credit score to get more cards, get the best rates for a mortgage, and negotiate better terms for a car loan. You can start playing around with balance transfer cards, retail cards, 0 percent APR cards, and so on.

With time, you will become an expert. You will see yourself, as I did, planning exactly when to apply for a new card. Friends will come to you asking for advice or your thoughts on a new card that just hit the market. Family members or significant others will start playing the game with you, becoming your "player two." This will help you maximize miles and multiply points. You will keep cards with no annual fee open just to help you age your credit. And to keep track of all your cards, you will have a system to stay on top of your spending, bonus, dates, points, and more. Finally, you will be referring your friends to cards with your referral link racking up points for the both of you. Right now, credit cards will hardly be an enemy.

I would love for you to help me help others with building their credit. I believe everyone should start their financial journey and reach their financial freedom. Do you think this book will help them? *Freedom in Credit Cards* is about more than credit cards. It's about being financially literate and sharing it with others. To keep up to date on new cards, sign-up bonuses, and get more resources, find me at LuccianoDiazSkoff.com. Or write me at Instagram @LuccianoDiazSkoff.

One last thing: Send me an email at lucciano@freedomincreditcards.com with the subject line: credit is a tool, and let me know what you learned from this book. I'd love to hear from you.

Acknowledgments

———

This book came to life out of the necessity that my friends and I had to learn about credit, to understand why our family members had debt, and to know how we can take charge of our credit cards and our life. It came to life when I got denied my first mortgage for my lack of credit and the apparent lack of financial literacy and the importance of building credit. This is the result of endlessly reading articles to make sure my next decision was the right one; the result of trial and error and my personal credit building journey.

I've helped countless friends and colleagues start their credit journey; get approved for their second, third, or fourth card; increase their chances to obtain better loan interest; and made the money conversation normal amongst us. This book has given me the chance to sit down with my parents and talk about their finances. It also brought me my biggest joy: helping them pay off $60,000 of debt completely.

The best part of this book for me is I get to acknowledge everyone who has helped me along the way and who has helped me get this done. And I get to thank those who volunteered as guinea pigs.

One very close friend thought I should write this book before it even occurred to me. Thank you, Miguel Hernandez, for suggesting I write this book in every conversation and making sure it happened.

Thank you to Jayson Ramos for introducing me to Eric Koester and the team of New Degree Press. Thank you, Eric and NDP team, for making all of this possible. Thank you to my editors, Jordan Waterwash and Cynthia Tucker, for patiently waiting on my manuscript and edits.

Thank you to Ulises Perez for the support since day one of writing this book and the restless support on the project.

Thank you to Gautam Shamdasani for the insight in credit and for answering countless questions at 3:00 a.m.

Thank you to everyone who supported me in the campaign and for making the book come true: Nicole Rubí Figueroa Encarnación, Alma Frontera, Miguel Hernandez, Annette Diaz, Juan Santiago, Carlos Ayala, Whitney Stewart, Adriana Camille Cabán Ureña, René Cotto, Jorge Cardona López, Carlos Aldarondo, Natalia Bellaflores, Christian López Camacho, Debora Aponte Martinez, Alex Sierra Bello, Leishla Agosto, Carla Camacho, Mario Castillo Acosta, Pedro Cruz, Gautam Shamdasani, Viviana Currais, Gabriella Perales, Brianna K Crane, Ana Maria Rodes Portelles, Christopher Russe Muniz, Jesus Edgardo Arroyo Quevedo, Edwin T De La Rosa, Ana Celeste Colón, Gianrene Padilla, Camila Alonso Conty, Valerie Mercado, Patrick Cleary, Amy Acevedo, Ulises Perez, Anthony Pabón Montañez, Juan Fernandez Melendez,

Amin Ganjalizadeh, Rogelio J Fernandez Serralles, Mark Chella, Dagoberto Montoya, Natalia Arelys Pagán Pérez, Fernando Herrero, Xavier Perez, Filex Rosado, Néstor Deliz, Adrian Figueroa, José Juan Russe-Russe, Jose F Soto, Susej Sánchez, Reinaldo Santos, Manuel Curet, Rubhí Garcia, Armando Seguí, Bryant Guardado, Manuel Kortright, Alberto Perez, John Roman-Santiago, Anneliz Oliver, Michael Burn, Maria Jaunarena, Kristian Ramirez, Angel Cintron, Angel E Cintron Jimenez, Ivan Cirino Simonet, Rafael Gutierrez, Leandro Diaz, Orlando Gonzalez, Gustavo Altieri, Natalia Coriano, Phillip Klumper, María del Mar Rivera, Michael Menda, Etienne Von, Alan Taveras, Luis Irizarry, Andrea Otero Mattei, H. Caro & Co., Luis H Rodriguez, Leamsi Fontánez, Daniela Santiago, Ing. Hector Colon De La Cruz, Cynthia Tucker, Kevin Perez Colon, Tatiana Velez, Juan G. Balsa, José Romero, and Fernando Mercado.

Thank you to all my friends who knowingly let me test the credit building techniques with them. Thank you to all my friends for your endless supply of credit card stories.

Immense gratitude to my family—Mary Jane, Walter, and Gustavo—for supporting me always. Thank you for being incredible role models and amazing parents and brother. And thank you to my grandparents—Carmen and Jake, Santiago and Rosa—who look after me wherever they are, *les pido la bendición.*

Special thank you to everyone who made this book a wonderful adventure.

Finally, to my readers. I hope this book helps you build your credit and start your journey to financial freedom.

Appendix

————

CHAPTER 1

DeMatteo, Megan. "This Is the Credit Score Lenders Use When You Apply for a Mortgage." CNBC. December 2, 2020. https://www.cnbc.com/select/which-credit-score-used-when-applying-for-mortgage/

Glink, Ilyce, and Samuel J Tamkin. "Perspective | The Key to Escaping from Debt Is to Pay off the Highest Interest Accounts First." *The Washington Post*. WP Company. March 13, 2020. https://www.washingtonpost.com/business/2020/03/16/key-escaping-debt-is-pay-off-highest-interest-accounts-first/

Irby, LaToya. "Find out How Long It Takes to Get Approved for a Credit Card." The Balance. June 14, 2020. https://www.thebalance.com/credit-card-application-approval-notice-960004

Lembo-Stolba, Stefan. "What Is the Average Credit Score in the U.S.?" *Experian*, September 6, 2019. https://www.experian.com/blogs/ask-experian/what-is-the-average-credit-score-in-the-u-s/.

CHAPTER 2

Gordon, Taylor. "How Much Is the Average Real Estate Commission?" Ownerly. June 18, 2020. https://www.ownerly.com/real-estate/average-commission-for-real-estate-agent/

CHAPTER 3

"35 Essential Auto Loan Statistics (2020 Update)." PolicyAdvice. December 7, 2020. https://policyadvice.net/insurance/insights/auto-loan-statistics/

"90% Of Global Data Was Created in the Last 2 Years—IBM." Optigra. November 6, 2014. https://optigra-soft.com/90-of-global-data-was-created-in-the-last-2-years-ibm/

"Credit: Definition of Credit by Oxford Dictionary on Lexico.com Also Meaning of Credit." Lexico Dictionaries | English. Lexico Dictionaries. Accessed December 30, 2020. https://www.lexico.com/definition/credit

Desjardins, Jeff. "The History of Consumer Credit in One Giant Infographic." *Visual Capitalist*, August 29, 2017. https://www.visualcapitalist.com/history-consumer-credit-one-infographic/

Gonzalez-Garcia, Jamie, and Allie Johnson. "Credit Card Ownership Statistics." *CreditCards.com*, January 15, 2020. https://www.creditcards.com/credit-card-news/ownership-statistics/.

Horch, AJ. "Almost Half of America Is Now Carrying Credit Card Debt, and More of It." CNBC. May 4, 2020. https://www.cnbc.com/2020/05/04/almost-half-of-america-now-carrying-credit-card-debt-and-more-of-it.html.

KIRKHAM, ELYSSA. "Personal Loan Statistics." LendingTree January 24, 2020. https://www.lendingtree.com/personal/personal-loans-statistics/

Kossman, Sienna. "The History of Credit Cards: Ancient Times to Present Day." *The Balance*, August 8, 2019. https://www.thebalance.com/history-of-credit-cards-4766953

MacDonald, Jay, and Taylor Tompkins. "The History of Credit Cards (Timeline & Major Events)." *CreditCards.com*, July 11, 2017. https://www.creditcards.com/credit-card-news/history-of-credit-cards/

Mastercard Brand History | Logo Evolution. Accessed December 30, 2020. https://brand.mastercard.com/brandcenter/more-about-our-brands/brand-history.html

Neal, Michael. "Mortgage Debt Has Peaked. Why Has the Share of Homeowners with a Mortgage Fallen to a 13-Year Low?" Urban Institute. August 20, 2019. https://www.urban.org/urban-wire/mortgage-debt-has-peaked-why-has-share-homeowners-mortgage-fallen-13-year-low

Orman, Suze. "Suze Orman's (Ridiculously Easy) Financial To Do List." January 2010. https://www.oprah.com/money/suze-ormans-financial-to-do-list-money-advice/2.

SoFi. "A History of Credit (and How to Manage Yours Better)." *SoFi*, February 3, 2017. https://www.sofi.com/learn/content/personal-loan-history-of-credit-cards/?__cf_chl_jschl_tk__=526078b1229a4af90ee28bd040a28881f2f-9b70c-1588292219-0-AcbdMcPMBWxx1Kh_Ki_wszQnaFVO-Jnuc89a3vhgHtDrVu-RBBiFWgBhJA3BjbXp1mPdjIxSiHC-bxijpy79cWQJvVKwz2_9svACweCT1W8ccT25PbFIOu-5181Q6eG8baClqZmH_6Bcv9wFrIPHIAULKOIKhV1b_G5ez-K_6UDwX-GsuomHyg2s02ax58t6QdxrkwoeiHe76D5nmUY-wqe75AZoA3d9ehPhYno-M6vkS4KXT9CR4gsB385piUFvd-

9JZIztOU7oJAzgHSu136x7Fqy-DVO_L1ExLKlvY1T0aL98l_
qs0aNtVFYfa_fp27RLWEGEpQnfFyjBnS7UeWfNav6Z9E-
go3MsGdVd6Jd3uDuhoeFtSkUtuHTyKE3VUnINSPqK-
MOoUYnqZs5zsxafvoxu7IM.

"The Consumer Credit Card Market." *Consumerfinance.
gov*, December 2015. https://files.consumerfinance.
gov/f/201512_cfpb_report-the-consumer-credit-card-mar-
ket.pdf.

"Using Consumer Reports for Credit Decisions: What to Know
About Adverse Action and Risk-Based Pricing Notices."
Federal Trade Commission. July 16, 2020. https://www.ftc.
gov/tips-advice/business-center/guidance/using-consum-
er-reports-credit-decisions-what-know-about-adverse

CHAPTER 4

"How Are FICO Scores Calculated?" myFICO. November 19,
2019. https://www.myfico.com/credit-education/whats-
in-your-credit-score

"How New Credit Impacts Your Credit Score." myFICO.
Accessed December 30, 2020. https://www.myfico.com/
credit-education/credit-scores/new-credit

"How Owing Money Can Impact Your Credit Score." myFICO.
Accessed December 30, 2020. https://www.myfico.com/
credit-education/credit-scores/amount-of-debt

"How Payment History Impacts Your Credit Score." myFICO.
Accessed December 30, 2020. https://www.myfico.com/
credit-education/credit-scores/payment-history

"How the Length of Your Credit History Impacts Your FICO
Score." myFICO. Accessed December 30, 2020. https://

www.myfico.com/credit-education/credit-scores/length-of-credit-history

" "How to Improve Your Credit Score." eLoan. Accessed September 18, 2020. https://www.eloan.com/blog/personal-finance/how-to-improve-your-credit-score#:~:text=If%20you%20don't%20take,and%2C%20ultimately%2C%20paying%20more.

"How Your Apple Card Application Is Evaluated." *Apple Support*, June 29, 2020. https://support.apple.com/en-us/HT209218

Mondalek, Alexandra. "Man Has Almost 1,500 Credit Cards and Near-Perfect Credit Score | Money." Time. January 4, 2016. https://time.com/4166577/guinness-record-credit-card-holder/

myFICO. "Credit Checks: What Are Credit Inquiries and How Do They Affect Your FICO Score?"Accessed October 9, 2020. https://www.myfico.com/credit-education/credit-reports/credit-checks-and-inquiries.

O'Shea, Bev. "How Does a Late Payment Affect Your Credit?" NerdWallet. December 16, 2020. https://www.nerdwallet.com/article/finance/late-bill-payment-reported

Pinsker, Beth. "A Doctor on TV, Hill Harper Is a Money Guru in Real Life." Reuters. May 13, 2019. https://www.reuters.com/article/us-money-lifelessons-hillharper/a-doctor-on-tv-hill-harper-is-a-money-guru-in-real-life-idUSKCN1SJ11E.

Resendiz, Joe. "How Credit Card Companies Make and Earn Money." ValuePenguin. December 12, 2019. https://www.valuepenguin.com/how-do-credit-card-companies-make-money.

"Types of Credit and How They Affect Your FICO Score." myF-ICO. Accessed December 30, 2020. https://www.myfico.com/credit-education/credit-scores/credit-mix

CHAPTER 5

Egan, John. "Credit Card Companies: What You Should Know." Credit Karma. January 12, 2021. https://www.creditkarma.com/credit-cards/i/what-to-know-about-credit-card-companies.

Mulcahy II, Michael. "Fraught with Fraud: Tips for Increasing Your Digital Security." Kings Path Partners. April 3, 2020. https://www.kingspath.com/fraught-with-fraud/.

Ramsey, Dave, and Sharon Ramsey. *Financial Peace Revisited.* New York: Viking, 2003.

"U.S. Department of the Treasury." Remarks by Secretary Henry M. Paulson, Jr. on Financial Rescue Package and Economic Update. December 14, 2020. https://www.treasury.gov/press-center/press-releases/Pages/hp1265.aspx.

"What Is a Cooperative?" ICA. Accessed December 30, 2020. https://www.ica.coop/en/cooperatives/what-is-a-cooperative

CHAPTER 6

Banton, Caroline. "How Underwriters Assess the Risk of Insurers." *Investopedia*, September 10, 2020. https://www.investopedia.com/terms/u/underwriting.asp

"Evan Esar Quote." AZQuotes. Accessed August 18, 2020. https://www.azquotes.com/quote/1082159.

"Mahatma Gandhi." Oxford Reference. Accessed September 19, 2020. https://www.oxfordreference.com/view/10.1093/acref/9780191843730.001.0001/q-oro-ed5-00004716.

Murphy, Chris B. "How Lenders and Banks Use Your Debt-to-Income (DTI) Ratio." *Investopedia*, September 22, 2020. https://www.investopedia.com/terms/d/dti.asp

CHAPTER 7

Adams, Dia. "American Express Centurion Black Card 2020 Review." Forbes. Forbes Magazine. July 21, 2020. https://www.forbes.com/advisor/credit-cards/reviews/centurion-from-american-express/.

"Forbes Quotes." Forbes. Forbes Magazine. Accessed September 19, 2020. https://www.forbes.com/quotes/7311/.

Holzhauer, Brett, Brett Holzhauer, and Brett Holzhauer is Value-Penguin's travel rewards expert. "J.P. Morgan Reserve Card (Formerly Chase Palladium): Everything You Need to Know." ValuePenguin. Accessed December 30, 2020. https://www.valuepenguin.com/jp- -reserve-card-chase-palladium.

O'Shea, Bev. "How Does a Late Payment Affect Your Credit?" NerdWallet. December 16, 2020. https://www.nerdwallet.com/article/finance/late-bill-payment-reported

Press, Associated. "Billionaire Earns First-Class Travel for Life by Putting Modigliani Nude on Amex." The Guardian. Guardian News and Media. November 24, 2015. https://www.theguardian.com/world/2015/nov/24/billionaire-earns-first-class-travel-for-life-by-putting-modigliani-nude-on-amex

"Robert Kiyosaki Quote." AZQuotes. Accessed October 19, 2020. https://www.azquotes.com/quote/756792.

Sethi, Ramit. *I Will Teach You to Be Rich: No Guilt, No Excuses, No BS - Just a 6-Week Programme That Works.* New York: Workman, 2020.

CHAPTER 8

"10 Famous Quotes About Finances & Credit." Credit One Bank. Accessed August 19, 2020. https://www.creditonebank.com/articles/10-famous-quotes-about-finances-credit#:~:text=~Oscar%20Wilde~&text=Wilde%20makes%20the%20point%20that,means%20you%20owe%20them%20money.

DeMatteo, Megan. "Baby Boomers Have an Average of $25,812 of Debt, Not Including Mortgages-Here's How They Compare to Other Generations." CNBC. CNBC, December 2, 2020. https://www.cnbc.com/select/how-much-debt-do-baby-boomers-have/

Emerson, Ralph Waldo. *The Complete Works.* New York and Boston: Houghton, Mifflin, 1904; Bartleby.com, 2013.

Holzhauer, Brett. "Amex Application Rules—What You Need to Know Before Applying for an Amex Credit Card." ValuePenguin. November 21, 2020. https://www.valuepenguin.com/amex-application-rules

"Millennials Worry More about Credit than Older Adults." CreditCards.com, August 17, 2020. https://www.creditcards.com/credit-card-news/millennials-worry-about-their-credit/

Resendiz, Joe. "Credit Card Usage and Ownership Statistics (2019 Report)." ValuePenguin. ValuePenguin, December 17, 2019. https://www.valuepenguin.com/credit-cards/statistics/usage-and-ownership.

Steinberg, Ethan. "The Ultimate Guide to Credit Card Application Restrictions." The Points Guy. May 20, 2020. https://thepointsguy.com/guide/credit-card-application-restrictions/

CHAPTER 9

Advocacy, Office of. "Small Businesses Generate 44 Percent of U.S. Economic Activity." SBA's Office of Advocacy. Accessed December 30, 2020. https://advocacy.sba.gov/2019/01/30/small-businesses-generate-44-percent-of-u-s-economic-activity/

"Business Credit Card Statistics." CreditCards.com. May 6, 2019. https://www.creditcards.com/credit-card-news/business-credit-card-statistics/

Hoover, Herbert. *Public Papers of the Presidents of the United States: Herbert Hoover: Containing the Public Messages, Speeches, and Statements of the President, March 4, 1929 to ... March 4, 1933*. Washington, D.C.: Office of the Federal Register, National Archives and Records Services, General Services Administration, 1974.

Pilon, Annie. "What Is a DUNS Number Used For?" Small Business Trends. July 10, 2020. https://smallbiztrends.com/2020/05/what-is-a-duns-number-used-for.html#:~:text=Your%20DUNS%2C%20on%20the%20other,widely%20used%20throughout%20the%20world.

Podcast, BiggerPockets Real Estate. How to Become a Millionaire Through Real Estate by Age 26. December 26, 2020. https://www.biggerpockets.com/blog/biggerpockets-podcast-316-millionaire-real-estate-26-graham-stephan

Tsosie, Claire. "6 Major Differences Between Business and Personal Credit Cards." NerdWallet. June 11, 2020. https://www.nerdwallet.com/article/credit-cards/major-differences-business-credit-cards-personal-credit-cards

CHAPTER 10

Brownson, Jeffrey. "What Is Credit Card Churning?" Forbes. Forbes Magazine. December 8, 2020. https://www.forbes.com/advisor/credit-cards/what-is-credit-card-churning/

Bucci, Steve. "How Closed Account Affects Credit Score." CreditCards.com. May 28, 2020. https://www.creditcards.com/credit-card-news/closed-accounts-credit-score-1586/#:~:text=Summary-,Closing%20a%20credit%20card%20account%20can%20hurt%20your%20score%20by,your%20length%20of%20credit%20history.

Dixon, Amanda. "The Pros and Cons of Credit Card Churning." SmartAsset. July 9, 2018. https://smartasset.com/credit-cards/the-pros-and-cons-of-credit-card-churning

Hurd, Erin. "Should I Try Credit Card Churning?" NerdWallet. July 29, 2020. https://www.nerdwallet.com/article/credit-cards/credit-card-churning.

Kerr, Richard. "The Ultimate Guide to Chase's 5/24 Rule." *The Points Guy*, May 1, 2020. https://thepointsguy.com/guide/ultimate-guide-chase-5-24-rule/

Reyes, Nick "Manufactured Spending Complete Guide." December 16. 2020. https://frequentmiler.com/manufactured-spending-complete-guide/

Tobias, Andrew. "Chapter Checklist Financial Needs What About a Loan." *American Way*, November 1982.

CHAPTER 11

Black, Michelle L. "The Safe Way to Cancel a Credit Card." *Investopedia*, May 20, 2020. https://www.investopedia.com/how-to-cancel-a-credit-card-4590033

Kiernan, John S. "Derogatory Credit: What It Means & How to Avoid It." WalletHub. February 21, 2016. https://wallethub.com/edu/d/derogatory-credit/19460.

Morgan, Emily. "Credit Repair - DIY vs Professional Help." Fit My Money, November 24, 2020. https://fitmymoney.com/credit-repair/.

Williams, Fred O. "How to Cancel a Credit Card Without Hurting Your Credit Score." CreditCards.com, December 10, 2020. https://www.creditcards.com/credit-card-news/help/cancel-credit-card-6000/.

CHAPTER 12

DeNicola, Louis. "How Often Should I Check My Credit Score?" Experian. December 9, 2020. https://www.experian.com/blogs/ask-experian/how-often-should-i-check-my-credit-score/.

Egan, John. "What to Do If Your Credit Limit Decreases." *Experian*, April 23, 2020. https://www.experian.com/blogs/ask-experian/what-to-do-if-your-credit-limit-decreases/.

Mish. "Consumer Credit Declines an Amazing $68.7 Billion." *Mish Talk*, June 5, 2020. https://www.thestreet.com/mishtalk/economics/consumer-credit-declines-an-amazing-68-7-billion.

Nelson, Jennifer. "A Drop in Your Card's Credit Limit Is Bad News for Your Credit Score—Here Are 8 Reasons It Could Happen, and What You Can Do to Fix It." *Business Insider*, March 16, 2020. https://www.businessinsider.com/personal-finance/what-to-do-credit-line-decrease.

O'Shea, Bev. "What Is the Highest Credit Score? Can You Get a 'Perfect' Score?" NerdWallet. December 16, 2020. https://www.nerdwallet.com/article/finance/highest-credit-score.

Porche, Brady. "Credit Card Limit Decreased? Why It Happens, and What to Do about It." *CreditCards.com*, August 28, 2020. https://www.creditcards.com/credit-card-news/credit-limit-decrease/

CHAPTER 13

Akin, Jim. "What Is a Charge-Off?" Experian. Experian, July 22, 2019. https://www.experian.com/blogs/ask-experian/what-is-a-charge-off/

Brady, Written by Sarah, Clint Proctor, Jennifer Brozic, CPA Erica Gellerman, John Egan, and Sean Bryant. "What Is a FICO Auto Score and What Score Is Good?" Credit Karma. December 8, 2020. https://www.creditkarma.com/auto/i/fico-auto-scores

Chase. Accessed December 31, 2020. https://www.chase.com/personal/credit-cards/education/interest-apr/how-to-calculate-credit-card-apr-charges.

Cornfield, Jill. "Your Credit Score Could Mean as Much as $45,000 in Savings... or Expenses." CNBC. CNBC, July 23, 2018. https://www.cnbc.com/2018/07/23/a-mediocre-credit-score-could-mean-paying-thousands-of-extra-dollars.html.

Crowe, Aaron. "How Do Debt Collection Agencies Work?: Everything You Need to Know." *Better Credit Blog | Credit Help for Bad Credit*, August 6, 2020. https://bettercredit-blog.org/collection-agencies/

Detweiler, Gerri. "How Much Will My Credit Score Drop If I Apply for a Car Loan?" Credit.com. April 16, 2018. https://www.credit.com/blog/how-much-will-my-credit-score-drop-if-i-apply-for-a-car-loan-111720/

Fontinelle, Amy. "How the Debt Collection Agency Business Works." *Investopedia*, May 26, 2020. https://www.investo-pedia.com/articles/personal-finance/121514/how-debt-collection-agency-business-works.asp.

Gravier, Elizabeth. "Filing for Bankruptcy Can Cause a Good Credit Score to Drop at Least 200 Points-Here's What You Should Know." CNBC. December 2, 2020. https://www.cnbc.com/select/how-long-do-bankruptcies-stay-on-credit-report/.

Heakal, Reem. "What Are the Forces Behind Interest Rates and What Causes Them to Rise?" *Investopedia*, August 5, 2019. https://www.investopedia.com/insights/forces-be-hind-interest-rates/

KAPFIDZE, TENDAYI. "LendingTree Reveals How Buying a House Affects Credit Scores." LendingTree, October 31, 2018. https://www.lendingtree.com/home/mortgage/credit-score-recovery-after-buying-a-home/

Knueven, Liz. "Here's the Average Auto Loan Interest Rate by Credit Score, Loan Term, and Lender." Business Insider. Business Insider, December 8, 2020. https://www.businessinsider.com/personal-finance/average-auto-loan-interest-rate.

O'Brien, Sarah. "Buying a House Can Send Your Credit Score down. Here's How Long It Takes to Recover." CNBC. November 6, 2018. https://www.cnbc.com/2018/11/06/buying-a-house-can-depress-credit-scores-how-long-it-takes-to-recover.html

"Resources." Factual Data. Accessed December 31, 2020. https://www.factualdata.com/products/resources/.

"Sample Letters to Dispute Information on a Credit Report." *Consumer Financial Protection Bureau.* Accessed October 12, 2020. https://www.consumerfinance.gov/consumer-tools/credit-reports-and-scores/sample-letters-dispute-credit-report-information/.

Sandford, Gideon. "How Do Collections Affect Your Credit? Top 10 Questions Answered." Credit Sesame. www.creditsesame.com, May 22, 2020. https://www.creditsesame.com/blog/credit/collections-affect-credit-top-10-questions-answered/.

"What Should I Do When a Debt Collector Contacts Me?" *Consumer Financial Protection Bureau.* Accessed October 12, 2020. https://www.consumerfinance.gov/ask-cfpb/what-should-i-do-when-a-debt-collector-contacts-me-en-1695/.

White, Jennifer. "Multiple Inquiries When Shopping for a Car Loan." Experian. January 30, 2020. https://www.experian.com/blogs/ask-experian/multiple-inquiries-when-shopping-for-an-car-loan/.

CHAPTER 14

"2020 U.S. Credit Card Satisfaction Study." J.D. Power. August 20, 2020. https://www.jdpower.com/business/press-releases/2020-us-credit-card-satisfaction-study

"Facts + Statistics: Identity Theft and Cybercrime." Insurance Information Institute. Accessed July 21, 2020. https://www.iii.org/fact-statistic/facts-statistics-identity-theft-and-cybercrime.

Gonzalez-Garcia, Jamie, and Allie Johnson. "Credit Card Ownership Statistics." *CreditCards.com*, January 15, 2020. https://www.creditcards.com/credit-card-news/ownership-statistics/.

"Identity Theft Odds: Identity Theft Statistics: Reduce the Risk of ID Theft: IdentityForce." We Aren't Just Protecting You from Identity Theft. We Protect Who You Are. December 15, 2020. https://www.identityforce.com/blog/identity-theft-odds-identity-theft-statistics

LaPonsie, Maryalene. "10 Things to Do If Your Identity Is Stolen." *U.S. News & World Report*, August 12, 2020. https://money.usnews.com/money/personal-finance/family-finance/articles/things-to-do-after-your-identity-is-stolen.

Lemire, Christy Lemire. "Review: 'Identity Thief' Has No Charge." telegram.com. February 9, 2013. https://www.telegram.com/article/20130209/NEWS/102099931.

Papadimitriou, Odysseas. "Identity Theft: What It Is, How It Happens & the Best Protection." WalletHub, December 8, 2020. https://wallethub.com/edu/identity-theft/17120#:~:-text=spending%2Drelated%20fraud.-,How%20Does%20Identity%20Theft%20Happen%3F,Gate%20Univer-

sity%20College%20of%20Law.&text=They%20can%20
then%20use%20this,even%20assume%20your%20iden-
tity%20entirely.

"Puerto Rico Coffee History." A Cup Of Puerto Rico. November
15, 2017. https://acupofpuertorico.com/puerto-rico-cof-
fee-history-3/.

"Puerto Rico Coffee Roasters Alto Grande." Puerto Rico Coffee
Roasters. Accessed August 21, 2020. https://www.puer-
toricocoffeeroasters.com/our-brands/alto-grande/.

Savage, Maddy. "Sweden's Cashless Experiment: Is It Too Much
Too Fast?" NPR. NPR, February 11, 2019. https://www.npr.
org/2019/02/11/691334123/swedens-cashless-experiment-
is-it-too-much-too-fast.

" "Specialty Coffee Brands to Taste in Puerto Rico." Discover
Puerto Rico. Accessed September 5, 2020. https://www.
discoverpuertorico.com/article/specialty-coffee-brands-
to-taste-puerto-rico.

"Warning Signs of Identity Theft." *Consumer Information*,
February 19, 2019. https://www.consumer.ftc.gov/arti-
cles/0271-warning-signs-identity-theft.

Made in the USA
Columbia, SC
09 June 2021